Living in Hope

Larry Rice

©2024 Larry Rice. New Life Publications. All Rights Reserved. No part of this publication may be reproduced or transmitted in any form or by any means, electronic or mechanical, including photocopying, recording, or an information storage or retrieval system, without prior permission in writing from the publisher.

LIVING IN HOPE

BY

LARRY RICE
NLEC PUBLICATIONS

Table of Contents

1: Holding on to Hope	4
2: Experiencing Hope After Being Blown Over	18
3: Overcoming Hope Fatigue	34
4: Experiencing and Sharing Hope	54
5: Touching the Divine in an Age of Hopelessness	71
6: Singing the Songs of Hope Found in Revelation	88
7: Celebrating With Songs of Hope	100
8: Living in Hope	113
9: Maintaining Hope in Spite of the Circumstances	130
10: Receive God's Gift of Hope through Faith and Prayer	146
11: Planting the Seeds of Hope and Love	164
12: How to Have Hope When You Are at the End of Your Rope	182
13: When It Comes to Hope Where Is Your Head At?	199
14: Here's Hope	216
15: Living in Hope, Faith and Love	232
16: Finding Hope in Hopeless Dark Places	247
17: Jesus the Hope of Heaven	261

Holding on to Hope
Chapter 1

It was the sixth anniversary of New Life Evangelistic Center and instead of excitement and enthusiasm it seemed that discouragement, disillusionment and hopelessness had over-whelmed a majority of the staff. Many of the staff members were in their late teens or early twenties. I myself was in my late twenties but still had a lot to learn when it came to directing an ever-growing ministry like NLEC.

New Life as a total faith ministry meant that we had to make many personal sacrifices as we trusted God for the daily donations required to operate the ministry. At the same time we were taking the financial needs to the Lord daily in prayer. I was also seeing the staff leaving one by one. I would pray and pray and even declared at one point that it seemed that the more I prayed the more hopeless the situation became. Things appeared to be going downhill quickly, but I knew in the depths of my soul I had to keep on believing and have hope.

At the beginning of the year there had been fifty staff members actively at work. Then the pruning spoken of in John 15:2 began to take place. There were some days that year when I felt that trouble was coming from every direction. At times I was almost overwhelmed. Life started looking totally negative and hopeless. But I knew I had to keep on believing and could not let anger, hopelessness or a critical attitude take over.

Paul described some of the struggles he had in his ministry as a sentence of death within ourselves. This description is given in 2 Corinthians 1:9-10, "*Indeed, we felt that we had received the sentence of death. But that was to make us rely not on ourselves but on God who raises the dead. He delivered us from such a deadly peril, and He will deliver us. On Him we have set our hope that He will deliver us again.*"

During these early years at New Life Evangelistic Center we were also learning we could not trust in ourselves. We had to trust God for giving up wasn't an option.

Giving up wasn't an option. I had a wife and three small children. We had invested our savings and six years of our life in this ministry and besides I knew this is where God called me. In order to survive each day, I had to continue in spite of my feelings, to call on the Lord in prayer. I would let passages like Psalm 50:15 come to life within me. There God told me to "...*call upon Him, in the day of trouble"* and then He promised, "*I will deliver you, and you will glorify me.*"

People that I had grown to love and trust were turning against me. It would have been so easy for me to be overwhelmed as troubling times were destroying my joy until I had a crying need for encouragement. Peter gave me that encouragement in verses 6 & 7 of this first chapter of 1 Peter. There I saw I had joy and hope not only now in times of trouble but, because of the resurrection of Jesus Christ, I had been given this living hope of eternal life.

"*In this you greatly rejoice, though now for a little while you may have to suffer grief in all kinds of trials. These have come so that your faith—of greater worth than gold, which perishes even though refined by fire—may be proven genuine and may result in praise, glory and honor when Jesus Christ is revealed"* (1 Peter 1:6 & 7).

God was using this time of trials and suffering to teach me patience. He also was showing me how outbursts of anger and hopelessness were self destructive and that fear only contributed to the problem by producing further distrust.

I knew I had a choice. I could let hopelessness and unbelief take over or I could strive to accept the fact that, *"His divine power has given us everything we need for a godly life through our knowledge of him who called us by his own glory and goodness. Through these he has given us his very great and precious promises, so that through them you may participate in the divine nature, having escaped the corruption in the world caused by evil desires. For this very reason, make every effort to add to your faith goodness; and to goodness, knowledge; and to knowledge, self-control; and to self-control, perseverance; and to perseverance, godliness; and to godliness, mutual affection; and to mutual affection, love. For if you possess these qualities in increasing measure, they will keep you from being ineffective and unproductive in your knowledge of our Lord Jesus Christ. But whoever does not have them is nearsighted and blind, forgetting that they have been cleansed from their past sins"* (2 Peter 1:3-9).

I tried to remind the rest of the staff that in the season of troubles and hopelessness we are told to, *"Consider it pure joy whenever you face trials of many kinds, because you know that the testing of your faith develops perseverance. Perseverance must finish its work so that you may be mature and complete, not lacking anything"* (James 1:2-4).

I knew that in the season of trouble, we would become bitter, not better, if we didn't consider it pure joy knowing that these troubles which tested our faith would, if we remained steadfast, develop within us perseverance. **We had to keep on believing and have hope.**

A small group of NLEC staff members stood steadfast as they would meditate on

Lamentations 3:21-24, *"Yet hope returns when I remember this one thing; The Lord's unfailing love and mercy still continue, fresh as the morning, as sure as the sunrise. The Lord is all I have, and so in Him I put my hope."*

It was scriptures like that which helped us to keep on going. Then in 1 Peter 1:8 we read *"Though you have not seen Him, you love Him; and even though you do not see Him now you believe in Him and are filled with an inexpressible and glorious joy, for you are receiving the goal of your faith, the salvation of your souls."*

The practical advice for living a victorious life of hope goes on in 1 Peter 1:13-16, *"Therefore, prepare your minds for action; be self-controlled; set your hope fully on the grace to be given you when Jesus Christ is revealed. As obedient children do not conform to the evil desires you had when you lived in ignorance. But just as He who called you is holy, so be holy in all you do; for it is written: Be holy, because I am holy."*

To "be holy" meant to abide in the presence of the Living God. At this time of intense trials and tribulations I knew I had to surrender my life, my hope, and my dreams to the One who loved me and gave His life for me. I couldn't waddle in hopelessness and sin. Instead, I had to set my "hope fully on the grace to be given when Jesus Christ returns".

As more and more people left, I fell on my knees in the lobby of the NLEC headquarters and cried out, "Dear Jesus, I don't know what's going on but I want you and only you on the throne of my life."

The staff that remained would pray, fast and stayed in the scriptures daily. They were such an encouragement. They would share with the new believers in our midst the importance of remaining steadfast.

Even as we did this the financial needs continued, and people kept leaving. Some were not only leaving the ministry but were encouraging others to do the same. Yet those of us who remained were told, *"Do not be afraid of what you are about to suffer. I tell you, the devil will put some of you in prison to test you, and you will suffer persecution for ten days. Be faithful, even to the point of death, and I will give you the crown of life"* (Revelation 2:10).

This prison took many different forms. For some it was fear. For others it was hopelessness, frustration, and disappointment. But there was the promise of the crown of life. **We had to keep on believing and having hope.** As Satan attacked, we had to resist him steadfastly in the faith, "*...because you know that the testing of your faith develops perseverance. Perseverance must finish its work so that you may be mature and complete not lacking anything*" (James 1:3-4).

The remaining New Life staff had to use the sword of the Spirit and the shield of faith to quench every fiery dart of the evil one (See Ephesians 6:16-17). We had to remember that Satan had been defeated through the death and resurrection of Jesus Christ. Colossians 2:13-15 told us that, "*God made us alive with Christ. He forgave us all our sins, having canceled the written code, with its regulations, that was against us and that stood opposed to us; He took it away, nailing it to the cross. And having disarmed the powers and authorities, He made a public spectacle of them, triumphing over them by the cross."*

We had to keep on having hope Jesus would bring us through these difficult times as we believed that, *"They overcame him (Satan) by the blood of the Lamb (Jesus Christ) and the word of their testimony; they did not love their lives so much as to shrink from death"* (Revelation 12:11). We were promised that, *"He (or she) who overcomes will not be hurt at all by the second death"* (Revelation 2:11). *"So, fight the good fight of faith. Take hold of the eternal life to which you were called"* (1 Timothy 6:12).

Promise after promise is given to those who have hope and remain faithful in Revelation 2 and 3. In spite of these words of promise, it was so easy to get tired out, worn out and burned out as I battled the devil, the world, and my sinful flesh day after day. I had to keep on having hope and believing. That is why it was so critical that I kept my daily appointments with God. In those daily appointments I talked to God in prayer, I read and meditated on the Scriptures under the anointing and power of the Holy Spirit and beheld the wonders of His creation.

As time passed the reality of John 15:1-5 became a living reality at New Life Evangelistic Center. It was becoming clear that Jesus is the true vine and His Father is the gardener and that the fruit bearing branch He prunes clean, to make it more fruitful still.

This pruning had involved a majority of the young middle class Jesus people who had come to the New Life Evangelistic Center during its first five years of ministry. Now God was doing a new work. As I sought the Lord, along with the remaining leadership at New Life Evangelistic Center, Jesus showed us that we were to welcome everyone including the homeless, not only into the center for shelter, but also to join the staff.

With the passing of time not only did our Lord rebuild the New Life staff but he did it by equipping many of those who were previously homeless for service unto Him. As Romans 8:28 says, "...*we know that in all things God works for the good of those who love Him, who have been called according to His purpose.*"

Sometimes that purpose is difficult to understand. Just ask Job, who, although trying to live a God-fearing life, found himself going through unbelievable suffering. The book of Job clearly illustrates that as believers we must have hope, when going through the fiery trial of suffering, and remain steadfast in faith, entrusting ourselves to God who judges justly, just as Jesus did when He suffered (See 1 Peter 2:23-25).

In Revelation 3:12 we are told, "*Him who overcomes, I will make a pillar in the temple of my God.*" Then in verse 21 we read, "*To him (and her) who overcomes, I will give the right to sit with Me on My throne, just as I overcame and sat down with my Father on His throne.*"

Why do we see ourselves all too frequently as hopeless victims who think about giving up when through Jesus Christ, we are declared victors and over comers? (See Ephesians 1:4-14) The fact is we can either choose to be over comers of sin, the world and Satan through Christ or we can be overcome by them. Those who continue to refuse Christ, and His overcoming power will ultimately be cast into hell itself. (See Revelation 2:11; 3:5; 20:15; 21:8) There is no in-between, for you are either an over comer through Christ or overcome by sin, the devil and the world's system. *"This is the victory that has overcome the world, even our faith. Who is it that overcomes the world? Only he (and she) who believes that Jesus is the Son of God"* (1 John 5:4-5).

Those who keep on believing in God are doers of the word and not hearers only (James 1:22). They are on the front lines reaching out to the poor, the fatherless, widowed, hurting and homeless. Believers have hope and are those who are able to declare, *"Therefore we do not lose heart. Though outwardly we are wasting away, yet inwardly we are being renewed day by day. For our light and momentary troubles are achieving for us an eternal glory that far outweighs them all. So we fix our eyes not on what is seen, but on what is unseen. For what is seen is temporary, but what is unseen is eternal*" (2 Corinthians 4:16-18).

Whatever the circumstances may be, don't give up, my brothers and sisters. Hang on, have hope trusting God as He declares, "*Never will I leave you; never will I forsake you*" (Hebrews 13:5). Now be an overcomer, for Christ has declared, "*It is done. I am the Alpha and Omega, the Beginning and the End. To him who is thirsty I will give to drink without cost from the spring of the water of life. He who overcomes will inherit all this, and I will be his God and he will be My son*" (Revelation 21:6- 7). That is His promise to those who keep on having hope and believe.

To those who are overcome by sin, the devil and the world's system of hopelessness Christ goes on and says, "*But the cowardly, the unbelieving, the vile, the murderers, the sexually immoral, those who practice magic arts, the idolaters and all liars—their place will be in the fiery lake of burning sulfur. This is the second death"* (Revelation 21:8).

Now you must determine in your heart this day that no matter what you are going through you will not give up. **Stand on the promises of God's word and continue to have hope as you remain faithful, trusting in Him through the power of Jesus our Risen Lord and Savior.**

Exploring God's Word to Learn How to Keep on Having Hope

1. Please describe the pruning spoken of in John 15:2.

2. According to 1 Peter 1:6-7 how can you have joy and hope in times of trouble?

3. What are the things we need to add to our faith according to 2 Peter 1:3-9?

4. In what ways will Lamentations 3:21-24 help you to remain steadfast with hope in times of trouble?

5. What practical advice does 1 Peter 1:13-16 give you for living a victorious life of hope?

6. In Revelation 2:10 what do you see will be given to those who remain faithful even to the point of death?

7. Why must perseverance finish its work according to James 1:3-4?

8. What promises are given to those who overcome in Revelation 3:12, 21?

9. Who does 1 John 5:4-5 say overcome the world?

10. How is it we don't lose heart even though outwardly we are wasting away according to James 1:22?

Experiencing Hope After Being Blown Over
Chapter 2

All of us have had those times in life when we have felt that we were like a tree that has been cut down, blown over, and uprooted. In the back of the New Life Evangelistic Center headquarters in Overland, Missouri, there is a tree that has experienced just that.

Some years back this large oak tree after being blown over, sat on its side, uprooted. After being cut off about 8 feet above the ground, it was pulled upright and left that way.

As time passed that tree started to sprout again as described in Job 14:7 where it says, *"At least there is hope for a tree: If it is cut down, it will sprout again and its new sprouts will not fail."*

Now as the NLEC staff and those in its residential training program go out to the parking lot each day, they see this sprouted tree and are reminded that in spite of their past they also can start over again.

The book of Job is the story of a man who had it all and lost it all. When Job had uttered his wish to be like a tree he was at the point of total despair.

In Job 13:25-28, Job in the midst of his pain and hopelessness had cried out to God, *"Will you torment a windblown leaf? Will you chase after dry chaff? For you write down bitter things against me and make me reap the sins of my youth. You fasten my feet in shackles; you keep close watch on all my paths by putting marks on the soles of my feet. So man wastes away like something rotten, like a garment eaten by moths."*

Satan had cut loose on Job with both barrels. Job had lost all his possessions, his children, his reputation and everything he valued in life. **Job was worse than homeless.** His wife saw him covered with sores and told him to "...*curse God and die*" (Job 2:9).

Job's so called three friends, instead of helping him, only threw accusations at him.

At his lowest point Job cried out, "*He tears me down on every side till I am gone; he uproots my hope like a tree*" (Job 19:10).

New Life Evangelistic Center has its tree of hope behind its building to remind those who were homeless and uprooted that in spite of their past they can sprout again.

Job had lost it all but he still did not curse God. Many are ready to do just that if they lose their phone, their home, or their health.

In the midst of his misery, Job remembered the sprouting tree. He knew in the depths of his being that like a tree, he would live again, even if he was cut down. By faith and with hope Job cried out, "*I know that my redeemer lives, and that in the end he will stand on the earth. And after my skin has been destroyed, yet in my flesh I will see God; I myself will see him with my own eyes – I, and not another. How my heart yearns within me!"* (Job 19:25-27).

We see that Job's desire to "see" God fulfilled, as God speaks to him out of a storm. In Job chapters 38, 39, 40, and 41, we read one of the most extended monologues from God in the Bible as He proceeds to talk directly to Job.

During this time of interaction God uses His creation to relate truths to Job that no man could communicate. When God finished speaking Job cried out, *"My ears had heard of you but now my eyes have seen you. Therefore I despise myself and repent in dust and ashes"* (Job 42:5-6).

Like Job, even when we have been blown over by the adversities of life, to the extent we have been uprooted, we can start over with hope.

This starting all over involves repenting. Job declared that he despised who he had been and repented. Such repentance replants us in Christ Jesus and allows His spiritual hope to flow in us and through us.

Jesus said in Mark 11:21-23, "*Truly I say to you, whoever says to this mountain, 'be taken up and cast into the sea' and does not doubt in his heart, but believes that what he says is going to happen, it will be granted to him. Therefore I say to you, all things for which you pray and ask, believe that you have received them, and they will be granted you.*"

Repentance involves renouncing the mountain of sin that blew you over in the first place, and believing that Jesus Christ is now planting you in His love with hope that allows you to be His new creation.

Repenting like Job did, and being replanted in God's grace and hope has two parts. **First we must confess our sins** (Proverbs 28:13, 1 John 1:9). **Then we must confess our righteousness.** In 2 Corinthians 5:21, we discover that we are now sprouting a new life as the righteousness of God. "*He made Him who knew no sin to be sin on our behalf, so that* *we might become the righteousness of God in Him."*

As new creations in Christ we need more than just a sin consciousness of what blew us over and uprooted us. We need a new awareness of what it now means to be made new in Christ Jesus. *"If anyone be in Christ they are a new creation. The old has passed away and the new has come"* (2 Corinthians 5:17).

Just a few of the hundreds of scriptures which describes our hope and new creation in Christ Jesus include Ephesians 2:10 that says we are His workmanship. Then there is 1 Peter 2:9 that says we are a chosen race, royal priests, and a holy nation.

Matthew 5:13 says we are salt. Matthew 5:14 says we are light. The description of who we are as we are made alive in Christ, goes on and on throughout the New Testament.

As a new creation in Christ you are now complete. *"For in Him all the fullness of*

Deity dwells in bodily form and in Him you have been made complete and He is the head over all rule and authority" (Colossians 2:9-10).

When you have confessed your sins and received Jesus Christ as Lord of your life you can declare, "*...I have died to sin*" (Romans 6:2). "*...I have been baptized into Christ's death*" (Romans 6:3). "*...I have been raised from the dead to walk in newness of life*" (Romans 6:4).

In order to grasp the reality of what it means to walk in the newness of life we must increase our RPM's.

RPM's equals power in an engine. By increasing the speed of the engine the RPM's are increased and the power is also increased. If you desire more power and hope in your spiritual life, you must increase your "RPM's":

Read God's word (2 Timothy 2:15)
Pray without ceasing (2 Thessalonians 5:17)

<u>M</u>emorize and meditate the scriptures
(Psalm 119:11, Joshua 1:8)

Read the scripture, then ask the Holy Spirit to open up your mind and heart to who you now are as you have been replanted in Christ Jesus, and are sprouting as a new creation.

For example by **reading, praying, and meditating** on just the first three verses of Ephesians 1 you will discover hope as you realize you are:

1. A faithful saint in Jesus Christ (v.1)
2. You have grace and peace (v.2)
3. You are blessed with every spiritual blessing in the heavenly places in Christ (v.3)

By **reading, praying, and meditating** on Colossians 1:12-14 you will experience hope:

A. The Father has qualified you to share in the inheritance of the saints (v.12)

    B. You have been delivered from the domain of darkness and transferred to the kingdom of Jesus (v.13)
    C. You have redemption and the forgiveness of sins (v.14)

You might have friends and relatives like Job did, who will try to make you feel hopeless. That is why as you **R**ead, **P**ray, and **M**editate on the scriptures you must think the right thoughts (Proverbs 23:7) and realize that you have the mind of Christ (Philippians 2:5). This means you will strive to bring every thought captive to the obedience of Christ (2 Corinthians 10:5) and think on the right things (Philippians 4:8).

In order to maintain your hope it is important you strive to speak the words of hope knowing that death and life are in the power of the tongue (Proverbs 18:21). Your words of hope can flow into your life from the God of hope.

The Bible is the Book of Hope, flowing from the God of hope, in order to anchor you in a life of hope. *"Now may the God of hope fill you with all joy and peace in believing, so that you will abound in hope by the power of the Holy Spirit"* (Romans 15:13).

Finally as a new creation in Christ, rooted and grounded in His love and hope, do the right things. **Let God work through you to help others.** Share Jesus in word and deed with everyone you come in contact with.

The circumstances of the past may have blown you over, but you are now being replanted in the hope God gives in order that you may sprout for His Glory.

Let the God of Hope fill you with all joy and peace as you increase your RPM's by **Reading** God's word, **Praying** without ceasing, and **Meditating** on the scriptures. Then start thinking the right thoughts, speaking the right words and doing the right things. When you do this you will see our risen Lord Jesus give you hope far beyond what you can ask or think.

Explore the Scriptures and be Replanted in Hope

1. What hope did Job express a tree can have in Job 14:7?

2. How does Job express hope in the midst of his suffering in Job 19:25-27?

3. In what ways does God use creation to give Job hope in the midst of his suffering in Job 38, 39, 40 and 41?

4. How can we start over with hope?

5. What hope does Jesus give us in Mark 11:21-23?

6. List the two parts involved in repenting and being replanted in God's grace.

7. How do the following scriptures describe our hope as a new creation in Christ?
     a. 2 Corinthians 5:17:

     b. Ephesians 2:10:

     c. 1 Peter 2:9:

     d. Romans 6:4:

8. What RPM's are needed in your spiritual life in order to build your hope for the future?

9. In what way can you experience hope by directing your RPMs at Colossians 1:12-14?

10. How does maintaining hope require the speaking of words of hope?

Overcoming Hope Fatigue
Chapter 3

At a time when so many are losing hope to the extent that they have no real future before them, it is critical that we learn to apply Proverbs 23:18 in our personal lives now: *"Surely there is a future, and your hope will not be cut off."*

I am by nature an optimist. When the NLEC building at 1411 Locust was closed in April 2017 by the city of St. Louis we had hopes that New Life Evangelistic Center would ultimately prevail in the courts to reopen this building.

After seven years of hoping I must confess I was beginning to experience what psycho-therapist Lesley Alderman calls "hope fatigue." She developed this term to describe people like me who after a period of time start struggling with a "deficit of optimism."

Maybe at this time you are also experiencing hope fatigue. In spite of the cir-cumstances you have tried to have hope.

In 1 Thessalonians 1:3 (NIV) I found a formula to deal with hope fatigue when Paul said, "...*we remember before our God and Father your work produced by faith, your labor prompted by love, and your endurance inspired by hope in our Lord Jesus Christ.*"

The formula given here to overcome hope fatigue involves three steps that must be implemented through prayer.

1. "*Your work produced by faith.*" Unless my work and hope is produced by faith it will ultimately result in hope fatigue. I must never forget how much God loves me. With this in mind, I must pray asking our Risen Lord to show me what things I must do to pursue the goal set before me. As I do this I must believe God is leading me and remain faithful in letting His love flow through me. Even if He closes one door I must believe He will open another.

2. *"Your labor prompted by love." "God so loved the world He gave His only begotten Son"* (John 3:16). Now I must have a hope that is *"...sure that neither death nor life, nor angels nor rulers, nor things present nor things to come, nor powers, nor height nor depth, nor anything else in all creation, will be able to separate us from the love of God in Christ Jesus our Lord"* (Romans 8:38-39 ESV). As my work is prompted by the knowledge of God's love for me I can have hope in spite of the circumstances. Even if things don't work out the way I have planned, I can *"...know that for those who love God all things to work together for good, for those who are called according to His purpose"* (Romans 8:28).

3. *"Your endurance inspired by hope in our Lord Jesus Christ."* If I am feeling hope fatigue I must reexamine what is the basis for my hope. If it is my own efforts no wonder I would be getting tired out, burned out or worn out. My endurance must be the result of my hope in my Lord Jesus Christ.

He is the way, the truth and the life. Daily, I need to ask the Holy Spirit to show me how Christ "...*is able to do far more abundantly beyond all that we ask or think, according to the power at works within us*" (Ephesians 3:20).

Because Christ is risen, we have hope according to His power that works in us. This power is demonstrated through every seed that is planted and then resurrected into the wonderful plant with the purpose planned at the time of its creation. The Creator of all commands through His creation and the power of His word, "*Fear not, for I am with you; be not dismayed, for I am your God. I will strengthen you, I will help you; I will uphold you with my righteous right hand*" (Isaiah 41:10). The fact that God upholds us with His righteousness right hand tells us we do not need to accept hope fatigue. Present circumstances cannot suffocate our hope for a future. The resurrected Christ has provided for us a hope for the future both now and for all eternity.

The question is how do you apply this in your personal life when you encounter hope fatigue? Many engage in fight or flight. Psalm 143 shows us a better way. The Psalmist David is desperate. He cries out, *"Hear my prayer, O Lord; give ear to my plea for mercy; in your faithfulness answer me, in your righteousness!"* (verse 1). Like David, perhaps you feel like declaring, *"…my spirit faints within me; my heart within me is appalled"* (verse 4).

Not only does David identify with our needs but he also shares some very practical steps to live victoriously when we are experiencing hope fatigue. He says *"Hear my prayer, O Lord."* **The first step is to pray.** Then David says, *"I remember the days of old"* (verse 5). **The second step** for victoriously living, David says, **is recalling the situations God brought us through in the past when everything seemed hopeless.**

The third thing David would do was to **meditate not only on the promise of God's Word but also upon the wonders of His works.** This includes not only His miraculous intervention in times of hopelessness but also the works and wonders of His creation. Beholding the wonders of God's creation sparks a sense of awe within us as we taste, touch, smell, hear and see all that He has made. But the wonders of God's works go far beyond creation. *"For God so loved the world that He gave His one and only Son, that whoever believes in Him shall not perish but have eternal life"* (John 3:16). Think about it. God loves us so much that He gave us His only begotten Son, who died on the cross for our sins and conquered death through His resurrection.

The fact is that even though we know that the death of Jesus Christ has provided the solution for sin and His resurrected body opened the door to an eternal future for us in the presence of God, we still live in a very troubled world. This troubled world also invades regularly our inner world, robbing us of the reality that we have a future filled with hope. Paul awakens us to the future that hope provides in the midst of our present circumstances when he declared, *"We rejoice in the hope of the glory of God. Not only so, but we also rejoice in our sufferings, because we know that suffering produces perseverance; perseverance, character; and character, hope. And hope does not disappoint us, because God has poured out His love into our hearts by the Holy Spirit, whom He has given us"* (Romans 5:2-5).

If you have received Jesus Christ as Lord and Savior of your life, then receive the hope and the future He has provided for you. **This hope frees you to love and be loved.** For without the free flow of such love you will find yourself growing old in a lifeless world without hope for a future. Many people grow old not because of the hardening of the arteries, but because of a hardening of the heart? Time and hopelessness wear us down as we travel through this life. Yet when we have hope burning within. This keeps the hearts of love from hardening, *"We do not lose heart. Though outwardly we are wasting away, yet inwardly we are being renewed day by day"* (2 Corinthians 4: 16 NIV). The Message Bible expresses this verse in the following fashion: *"We're not giving up. How could* *we! Even though on the outside it often looks like things are falling apart on us, on the inside, where God is making new life, not a day goes by without His unfolding grace."*

As we are renewed inwardly daily we are assured of a "future filled with hope". It is in this knowledge by which hope fatigue is overcome. Yes, the needs may be mounting, but the reality that, "...*my God will meet all my needs according to His glorious riches in Christ Jesus*," (Philippians 4:19) provides a present peace and a hope for the future that passes all understanding.

Chances are you are already experiencing hope fatigue in whatever you are doing if you don't have your eyes fixed on Jesus and the hope of heaven. In AD 250, a man named Cypman had "his eyes fixed on Jesus" and possessed a hope that had a future. He wrote his friend Donatus:

"This is a cheerful world as I see it from my garden under the shadows of my vines. But if I were to ascend some high mountain and look out over the wide lands, you know very well what I should see: brigands on the highways, pirates on the sea, armies fighting, cities burning; in the amphitheaters men murdered to please applauding crowds; selfishness and cruelty and misery and despair under all roofs. It is a bad world, Donatus, an incredibly bad world. But I have discovered in the midst of it a quiet and holy people who have learned a great secret. They have found a joy, which is a thousand times better than any pleasure of our sinful life. They are despised and persecuted, but they care not. They are masters of their souls. They have overcome the world. These people, Donatus, are the Christians—and I am one of them."

Cyprian had a joy resulting in a hope that had a future. He had overcome the world to the extent that he later died for his newfound joy and the hope it produced. Yet even death could not rob him of this hope, for death itself provided the reality of heaven with an eternity in the presence of the Living God.

We may have found that as we have moved through life, pain and uncertainty. But **our willingness to endure suffering because of our love for others enables us to move closer to the heart of the divine.** As we get older, we discover that joy is often wedded to sorrow, and peace is given in the midst of pain. **Living the Christian life is a journey of faith**, which takes us everywhere we always wanted to go, but never by the route we expect or choose. Yet as we trust God, we receive a hope that has a future. This hope produces a powerful joy that cracks open the deepest sadness and disappointments of life because it is focused on Jesus our Risen Lord.

When Nehemiah told the people, "*...the joy of the Lord is your strength*" (Nehemiah 8:10) he was actually saying the joy of the Lord is your <u>wall</u>. It is this wall, which surrounds our souls and enables us to endure the paradox of pain because we have the hope of heaven and the eternal future that it provides. "*For in this hope we were saved. But hope that is seen is not hope* *at all. Who hopes for what he (or she) already has? But if we hope for what we do not yet have, we wait for it patiently"* (Romans 8:24-25).

To live in the hope that Christ provides is vital. This hope enables us to live fully in the now with the joy that God will be with us in whatever the future may bring. In the midst of their needs, the Biblical writers, who experienced this hope, were able to say *"...we have tasted of the goodness of the word of God and the powers of the coming age"* (Hebrews 6:5) and have already experienced *"...the Spirit as a deposit, guaranteeing what is to come"* (2 Corinthians 5:5). J. Moltmann points out that, "the one who is born again is, as it were, ahead of himself; he lives from the thing that is coming to him, not from what is already in him."

We have hope because God has called us to be more then conquerors through Jesus Christ who strengthens us. In Ephesians 6:10-12 we are told, *"...be strong in the Lord and in His mighty power.*

Put on the full armor of God so that you can take your stand against the devil's schemes. For our struggle is not against flesh and blood, but against the rulers, against the powers of the dark world and against the spiritual forces of evil in the heavenly realms."

We are involved in a spiritual battle in which we are called to be victors not victims. In 1 Timothy 1:18-19 we are told to "...*fight the good fight, holding on to the faith and a good conscience. Some have rejected these and so have shipwrecked their faith."*

Fighting the good fight is as the Lord told Zerubbabel in Zechariah 4:6, *"Not by might nor by power, but by my spirit, says the Lord Almighty."*

I have found in my daily battles that these words are so true. Satan will try to defeat me with depression, anxiety, and frustration and at times even hope fatigue. How I must remember that victory and the hope it provides is not through my own might or power but by the Spirit of God. This is illustrated in Revelations 12:10-11 where it says, *"Now have come the salvation and the power and the Kingdom of our God, and the authority of His Christ. For the accuser of our brothers, who accuses them before our God day and night has been hurled down. They overcame him by the blood of the Lamb and the word of their testimony."*

We are victorious over Satan as a result of the death of Jesus Christ (the shedding of His blood) and the power of His resurrection. The word of our testimony is the personal application of this "blood of the lamb" to the "door post" of our hearts. This takes us back to the Passover in Exodus 12:13 where God told the children of Israel, *"The blood will be a sign for you on the houses where you are; and when I see the blood, I will pass over you. No destructive plague will touch you when I strike Egypt."*

John the Baptist, in reference to Jesus, declared in John 1:29, *"Look, the Lamb of God, who takes away the sin of the world."* Paul describes the effects of the bloodshed on the cross by the *"Lamb of God"* (Jesus) in Ephesians 1:7-8,

Ephesians 2:13, and Colossians 1:20. In Ephesians 1:7-8 we read, *"In Him, we have redemption through His blood, the forgiveness of sins, in accordance with the riches of God's grace that He lavished on us with all wisdom and understanding."*

When Satan tries to depress and defeat us with thoughts and feeling of guilt, by putting on our helmet of salvation (Ephesians 6:17) and meditating on the fact that our sins have been forgiven because of the "blood of the Lamb" we have hope.

But there is more. As the evil one tries to make us feel alone, forsaken and hopeless we are able to defeat Satan by believing Ephesians 2:13. *"But now in Christ Jesus you who once were far away have been brought near through the Blood of Christ."*

For the one who lives in the hope that Christ provides there is a future. This hope is more than optimism that believes things will improve. It is a hope centered in God. It acknowledges that He loves us and is drawing us through the circumstances of life into His will and purpose for our lives. This reality births within us a hope that knows it is not us but God who has the final word and *"That in all things God works for the good of those who love Him, who have been called according to His purpose"* (Romans 8:28).

I would like to conclude with these words by Henri Nouwen:

"Zechariah, Elizabeth and Mary were not filled with wishes. They were filled with hope. Hope is something very different. Hope is trusting that something will be fulfilled, but fulfilled according to the promises and not according to our wishes. Therefore, hope is always open-ended."

"I have found it very important in my life to let go of my wishes and start hoping. It was only when I was willing to let go of wishes that something new, something beyond my own expectations could happen to me. Just imagine what Mary was actually saying in the words, 'I am the handmaid of the

Lord… let what you have said be done to me' (Luke 1:38). She was saying, 'I don't know what this all means, but I trust that good things will happen.' She trusted so deeply that her waiting was open to all possibilities. And she did not want to control them. She believed that when she listened carefully, she could trust what was going to happen."

"To wait open-endedly is an enormously radical attitude toward life. So is to trust that something will happen to us that is far beyond our own imaginings. So too, is giving up control over our future and letting God define our life, trusting that God molds us according to God's love and not according to our fear. The spiritual life is a life in which we wait, actively present to the moment, trusting that new things will happen to us, new things that are far beyond our own imagination, fantasy or predication."

The challenge that now exists for each of us is to overcome hope fatigue by knowing that we have a future filled with hope. Living in this hope, based upon the promises of God's word, involves a radical stance toward life where we surrender to Jesus Christ and His will for our lives.

Exploring the Bible and Discovering how to Overcome Hope Fatigue

1. What is the formula given in 1 Thessalonians 1:3 for dealing with hope fatigue?

2. What are the three steps David gives in Psalm 143:1-5 for living victoriously with hope?

3. How does Paul awaken us in Romans 5:2-5 to a hope for the future even though we may be suffering now?

4. Why is it so important we are renewed day by day according to 1 Corinthians 4:16?

5. How did Cypman express in 250AD that we can be master of our souls even in the midst of persecution?

6. What did Nehemiah mean in Nehemiah 8:10 that the joy of the Lord is your strength?

7. According to 1 Timothy 1:18-19 and Zechariah 4:6 how do we fight the good fight of faith?

8. Revelations 12:10,11 tells us that we overcome Satan by the blood of the lamb and word of our testimony. How is this done according to Ephesians 6:17 and 2:13?

9. What promise does Romans 8:28 give us that we have a hope and a future?

10. According to Henri Nouwen why is it important
       to let go of your wishes and start hoping?

Experiencing and Sharing Hope
Chapter 4

It is critical we experience hope and share it with others. When people lose hope they do desperate things. **People need hope.** That is why it is so devastating to tell that husband, or wife, son or daughter that they will never change. When you tell someone this you are taking away their hope. It is almost the same as shoving that person under water and telling them to breathe. People need hope to survive just like they need oxygen to breathe.

The hopeless are often the ones who engage in crime, commit suicide or murder. These are the people who have lost hope both now and for all eternity. Jesus came to set the captives of hopelessness free. That is why it is so tragic that many who profess to be His followers have let the hopelessness of legalism squeeze all life out of His message of hope.

These legalists have taken the free gift of eternal life that Christ provides and made it a promise that is impossible to obtain. The Bible is the ultimate manual for giving the necessary directions for bringing forth a revival of hope. The hope it gives is real hope, not political promises or hopeless legalism. It has provided hope both now and for all eternity.

The gospel is the message of good news that produces hope. It is hope for today, tomorrow, next week, next year and all eternity. This hope declares failure is not final.

From Genesis to Revelations, we see that hope springs eternal. The Bible spells out **B**asic **I**nstructions **B**efore **L**eaving **E**arth and gives one example after another of how ordinary human beings received hope and help from the God of hope.

In order for hope to take root in my life I must be a doer of the Word and not a hearer only (James 1:22). This means it's not good enough for me to just have a habit of reading the Bible. I must apply what I read by doing what it tells me. For example, when I am facing a hopeless situation I must first stop and then pray Philippians 4:13 that says, *"I can do all this through Him who gives me strength."* Then I must continue to move forth by faith.

It is reading and applying God's Word which enables you and I to receive hope and be overcomers. For example, as we read Psalms 121, we will see how help doesn't come from the mountains, whether it's people, circumstance or other things. Real help comes from our Living, Loving God, who is never asleep on the job. As we daily read and apply the scriptures hope will get down deep inside us and change our lives.

At the time he was in his thirties, Phil Thatcher had spent over half his life either in reform school or prison. It looked like Phil was going to be a career criminal until that day another prisoner tossed a worn-out Bible in Phil's cell. Out of curiosity, Phil started reading that Bible. As time passed, the Holy Spirit worked in Phil's life until he surrendered himself to Jesus Christ. It was then that Phil found a hope for his future that passed all under-standing. The Living

Lord had healed Phil to the extent that when the Parole Board freed him from prison, Phil spent the rest of his life telling everyone he met about the miracle God had worked in his life.

As we get in the habit of reading and applying the scriptures we see in Matthew 14:24-33, how Jesus gives hope in the storms of life. Filled with fear the disciples were so out of tune to the presence of Jesus that they thought He was a ghost when He came to them in the storm walking on the water.

Facing those storms in our life that are keeping us from experiencing the fullness of God (Ephesians 3:19) can be downright depressing. Psalm 51:17 goes on to say, "*My sacrifice, is a broken spirit: a broken and contrite heart you, God, you will not despise.*"

Jesus will heal our broken hearts and tell us, "*If you hold to my teaching, you are really my disciples. Then you will know the truth, and the truth will set you free*" (John 8:31-32).

Alister McGrath in his book, <u>Glimpsing the Face of God</u>, stated: "God has created us to relate to Him and, if we do not do so, we lose sight of our true goal and joy. We are designed to need God, as a computer is designed to run on electricity. God Himself would thus be the ultimate food and fuel of authentic human existence. God does not offer us salvation and joy as if these could somehow be detached from His loving caring presence. Without God, we are unfulfilled, precisely because we have been created with a God-shaped gap, within us, which cries out to be filled with the luxurious presence of our Creator. God has thus fashioned us in such a way that we may begin to gain at least a glimpse of His nature and being from the world around us."

As we absorb these wonders of creation, and desire the habits of the heart to be centered in God, let us not lose sight of the fact that the key to intimacy with the Holy Triune God lies in Jesus Christ. As 1 Peter 1:3-5 declares, *"Praise be to the God and Father of our Lord Jesus Christ! In His great mercy He has given us new birth into a living hope through the resurrection of Jesus Christ from the dead, and into an inheritance that can never perish, spoil or fade. This inheritance is kept in heaven for you, who through faith are shielded by God's power until the coming of the salvation that is ready to be revealed in the last time."*

Thank God for Jesus who *"has caused us to be born again to a living hope."* It is because of the death and resurrection of Jesus Christ you and I can experience hope both now and for all eternity.

By developing the habit of reading God's word daily we can see we are not destined for hell. Instead as children of God who have a hope that is certain we can know we will be with Him forever in heaven. It is the promises found in the Bible and the Holy Spirit working in our lives that gives us that certainty.

Our living Lord wants to show us how we can live victoriously as we develop the habit of reading the Bible every day. This takes place once we are convinced as Paul was of God's love. "*In all these things we are more than conquerors through Him who loved us. For I am convinced that neither death nor life, neither angels nor demons, neither the present nor the future, nor any powers, neither height nor depth, nor anything else in all creation, will be able to separate us from the love of God that is in Christ Jesus our Lord*" (Romans 8:37-39).

The love that God has for you, which is revealed throughout the Bible, provides the very foundation of hope. **The question is will you receive this love He has for you?** Satan is constantly trying to offer cheap substitutes for this eternal love that God provides. When one becomes sick and tired of such and desires God's love, then the enemy tries to make them feel they are not worthy of such. In order to combat Satan's lies and feeling of condemnation we must use the tools that the Word of God provides.

Let's study the tools of hope Jonah used to get out of the bottom of the whale's belly he found himself in. One of these tools Jonah used was the tool of prayer. Jonah declared, *"In my distress I called to the Lord, and He answered me. From deep in the realm of the dead I called for help, and you listened to my cry"* (Jonah 2:2).

It would have been so easy for Jonah to have lost hope as he sat in the belly of that fish. But he didn't give up, he gave his problem to God and said, *"...I will look again toward your holy temple"* (verse 4). Jonah chose in spite of the circumstances to hang on to hope and look to God even as he declared, *"The engulfing waters threatened me, the deep surrounded me; seaweed was wrapped around my head"* (verse 5). But that wasn't all. *"To the roots of the mountain I sank down; the earth beneath barred me in forever"* (verse 6).

It is in the Word of God that we receive the hope we need for being overcomers. Each and every day, we learn that the one thing about being at rock bottom is that the only place we can go from there is up. *"But you, Lord my God, brought my life up from the pit. When my life was* *ebbing away, I remembered you, Lord, and my prayer rose to you, to your holy temple"* (remainder of verse 6 and verse 7). As I read the Bible and see how Jonah spoke these words while he was still in the whale's belly, I am also encouraged to have hope and trust the Lord in spite of the circumstances.

From the bottom of the whale's belly, I am reminded that, *"those who cling to worthless idols turn away from God's love for them"* (verse 8). I frequently find myself saying Lord; I want that grace I read about in the Bible, so I hereby turn loose of those worthless idols. Jonah proclaimed, *"But I, with a shouts of grateful praise, will sacrifice to you. What I have vowed I will make good, I will say, 'salvation comes from the Lord'"* (verse 9). With that declaration, *"the Lord commanded the fish, and it vomited Jonah onto dry land* (verse 10).

In the midst of the belly of hopelessness we must daily read the Bible and believe God for deliverance. God is faithful and true to His Word. The hope God gives put Jonah back on track. God was then able to use him to call the people of Nineveh to repentance. Now as we trust God from the bottom of whatever "whale's belly" we might find ourselves in, and live in the hope he has given us, we can rest assured He will deliver us, as we believe that "*salvation comes from the Lord.*"

This salvation that comes from the Lord gives us the strength through the power of the Holy Spirit to give hope to the poor and homeless as we "*Speak up for those who cannot speak for themselves, for the rights of all who are destitute. Speak up and judge fairly; defend the rights of the poor and needy*" (Proverbs 31:8-9).

We are told in Psalms 82:3-4, "*Defend the weak and the fatherless; uphold the cause of the poor and the oppressed. Rescue the weak and the needy; deliver them from the hand of the wicked.*"

It is the knowledge of God's love revealed in the Scriptures that triggers within me the love to give hope to others as explained in 1 John 4:19-21. "*We love because He first loved us. Whoever claims to love God, yet hates a brother or sister is a liar. For whoever does not love his brother and sister, whom they have seen, can-not love God, whom they have not seen. And He has given us this command: Anyone who loves God must also love their brother and sister."

When I daily read the Scriptures, I discover I can let God's love and the hope it provides flow in me and through me into a hurting world. As I move by faith doing this, I become a living instrument proclaiming the love of Christ in word and deed. It is then I discover the hope which gives me additional strength to persevere in spite of the circumstances.

This hope is a result of daily reading the scriptures, and realizing *"If God is for us, who can be against us. He who did not spare His own Son, but gave Him up for us all – how will He not also, along with Him, graciously give us all things? Who will bring any charge against those whom God has chosen? It is God who justifies. Who then is the one who* *condemns? No one, Christ Jesus who died – more than that, who was raised to life – is at the right hand of God and is also interceding for us. Who shall separate us from the love of Christ? Shall trouble or hardship or persecution or famine or nakedness or danger or sword? As it is written: 'For your sake we face death all day long; we are considered as sheep to be slaughtered.' No, in all these things we are more than conquerors through Him who loved us. For I am convinced that neither death nor life, neither angels nor demons, neither the present nor the future, nor any powers, neither height nor depth, nor anything else in all creation, will be able to separate us from the love of God that is in Christ Jesus our Lord."* (Romans 8:31-39).

We must let God's Word come alive within us as we feel the pressures coming from every direction. Even the big bills, along with a host of other needs, won't seem that hopeless when we dwell upon the fact that *"if God be for us who can be against us?"* He didn't even spare sending His only begotten Son to provide redemption and freedom from sin, death and the devil. Now why should we doubt He will provide everything else we need?

In the midst of the storms of life, Jesus is there assuring us that **He has everything under control.** Experiencing hope is the result of being awakened daily to God's presence by praying and taking the Biblical medicine given in the scripture and observing His works of creation. As we do this we will have hope for Jesus has promised, "*Surely I am with you always to the very end of the age*" (Matthew 28:20).

Remember the secret for having hope and sharing it with others involves going to God's medicine cabinet daily and reading the Bible. As Joshua 1:8 & 9 (ICB) says, "*Always remember what is written in the Book of the Teachings. Study it day and night to be sure to obey every-thing that is written there. If you do this, you will be wise and successful in everything.*"

Tomorrow instead of being sick with worry, start out your day reading the Bible. There you will find hope in verses like Isaiah 41:10 (NCV) where it says "*Don't worry, because I am with you. Don't be afraid because I am your God. I will make you strong and will help you; I will support you with my right hand that saves you."*

At this moment determine in your heart and mind that you are not going to lose hope. Instead you will experience strength and healing from God's word as you hold firmly to the hope that you have in Jesus Christ. *"Now may the God of hope fill you with all joy and peace as you trust in him, so that you may overflow with hope by the power of the Holy Spirit"* (Romans 15:13).

Experiencing and Sharing Hope

1. How can it be said that the Bible is the manual for giving hope that gives us Basic Instructions Before Leaving Earth?

2. In order to live in hope why is it important we get in the habit of reading and applying scriptures?

3. What is the God-shaped gap within us and how can it be filled according to Alister McGrath?

4. What is the living hope and the inheritance spoken of in 1 Peter 1:3-5?

5. How does the love God has for us provide the very foundation of hope according to Romans 8:37-39.

6. Study carefully Jonah's prayer in Jonah 2:2-10. What steps does Jonah show in this prayer that we need to take when we are in the belly of a whale of hopelessness?

7. Why is it important we share hope with the poor and homeless according to Proverbs 31:89, Psalm 82:3 and 1 John 4:19-21?

8. According to Romans 8:31-39 how much does God love us?

9. How does knowing God loves you this much give you hope for the future?

10. In what ways will starting each day by observing God's creation and meditating on passages like Isaiah 41:10 and Romans 15:13 give you hope that day?

Touching the Divine in an Age of Hopelessness
Chapter 5

It is easy, in this hectic, dog eat dog world to lose all hope and feel that nobody really cares about us. Without hope it seems as if this world is growing more and more impersonal and colder with each passing day. So it comes as no surprise that we begin to feel like another nameless face in the crowd or another number lost in prison.

As we become victims of loneliness and hopelessness, life becomes meaningless. Our hopes for tomorrow, full of promises, seem to fade. We begin to feel like all the life in us has been bled away.

Today when many people put more trust in statistics than God, let's look at a woman who was hurting in Mark 5:25-34.

There we find a nameless, hopeless woman whom verses 25 and 26 describe as follows: "*Now a certain woman had a flow of blood for twelve years and had suffered many things from many physicians. She had spent all that she had and was no better, but rather grew worse."*

Sick and alone, a nameless face in a vast crowd, was this woman who desperately needed help. She was not satisfied with just getting close to Jesus.

She didn't want to just celebrate His presence. She was determined to touch Jesus because she was feeling hopeless.

Hopeless people do unusual things. Some engage in self-destructive activities like drugs, alcohol or the accumulation of materialistic things. They are people who are often lonely, living on the edge, who somewhere along the way have lost their purpose for living.

But not this woman. She had a purpose and she was going to accomplish it. She was going to touch Jesus at all costs. She was not satisfied with the Jesus whom crowds had seen. She was not interested in a Jesus who was an impersonal miracle worker or who only responded to the rich, the powerful, the strong, or those who dropped money in the collection plate. No, this woman knew the Christ of the scriptures. The Christ who reached out to the prostitute, the homeless, the despised leper, the condemned, the sick, the possessed and the nameless, hopeless, and the desperate.

She pushed her way through the crowd pushing and shoving people that got in her way. She had to touch Jesus. She was desperate. When He passed by she reached out and touched the edge of His garment.

Like an electric shock, there surged into the shrunken veins, the panting lungs, the withered muscles, Jesus' power and vitality! Recognizing the magnetic touch of faith amid the presence of the crowd, Jesus stopped and asked, "*Who touched me?*"

The question seemed ridiculous to the disciples. They answered, "How should we know there is such a crowd of people?" but Christ stopped, looked around, and gazed into the face of the desperate woman as He said to her, "Daughter your faith has made you well. Go in peace and be healed of your affliction."

This woman had no money, only faith! She met Him on the street, in a crowd. This name-less, hopeless woman had touched Jesus in desperate believing faith and He stopped! The fact is the touch of one hurting woman in a crowd halted the Lord of glory. She touched Him and so can we.

You might want to say, "That's impossible, God's not interested in me". Yes He is. Think about it, the one who conquered sin, death, and the devil stopped because one sick and hope-less woman touched Him. Yet there is even more. Jesus died and rose for you. As Romans 8 declares **there is no limit to His love.**

In this selfish and greedy world, we need to touch Jesus like never before. Oh how we need to touch Him. But we too often are like those in the crowd who are curious, seeking Him, even coming close to Him, but never actually touching Him. The fact is that this world is self-destructing and coming closer is not enough. It's like missing a plane by a few minutes or an hour, you still missed it.

Yes, we preach, pray, and say the creeds that set forth the hope that the Lord is near us, but we never actually touch Him nor experience the power He has promised. We need to ask ourselves this question: "How can I touch Jesus?"

You can begin by pouring out your hopelessness, hurt, and pain to the Lord in prayer. Push through the crowd of feelings and thoughts of unbelief. Believe that God will hear and that He will answer in a very special way. Start stepping out by faith as you wait for the answer.

Do what He tells you to do. Touch Jesus as He outlines His presence in Matthew 25:31-46. Help those in need. Then develop a growing conviction that He's waiting for you to touch Him.

Many are not touching Jesus because they refuse to stop believing they are born losers for whom there is no hope.

Moses was one of those you could say was a born loser. He was born a Jew in a land ruled by anti-Semitic people. Moses entered a world where his parents had to hide him to secure his life and then they had to release him to Pharaoh's daughter. His people were whipped, oppressed, hated, abused, misused and even murdered. The world that Moses entered was one of cruelty, pain and hopelessness.

At this time of hopelessness, ungodliness and injustice, Jesus promises in Matthew 28:20, *"Surely I am with you always, to the very end of the age."* Jesus hears, cares, and desires to touch you with His love.

In Exodus 3:7-8, God said to Moses, *"I have indeed seen the misery of my people in Egypt. I have heard them crying out because of their slave drivers, and I am concerned about their suffering. So I have come down to rescue them from the hand of the Egyptians..."*

God is always aware and He cares very deeply and will do whatever it takes to rescue you. Whether it is parting the Red Sea or closing the lion's mouth of hopelessness, God will make a way. He has promised He will never leave you nor forsake you. Now we must never forget the promise of Romans 8:37-39, *"We are more than conquerors through him who loved us. For I am convinced that neither death nor life, neither angels nor demons, neither the present nor the future, nor any powers, neither height nor depth, nor anything else in all creation, will be able to separate us from the love of God that is in Christ Jesus our Lord."*

It is no accident that you born at this time in history. **Remember the darker it seems the brighter your light can shine.** In the midst of such darkness God is looking for a man or a woman who will believe the fact they can touch Him by being more than conquerors through Christ who loves them.

Will you be that person of faith who will yield to God's will and seize the day for God's glory? You may feel unqualified, uneducated, unworthy and even one who was born in the most hopeless of circumstances. But if you truly believe that He is with you always even unto the end of the earth, nothing can separate you from the love of God and His divine truth. Now arise at this moment and have hope that your light will shine through your courageous acts of compassion and justice.

But what about those times in the past when you really believed, tried, trusted, stepped out by faith and then fell flat on your face? Now your memory of those moments hold you in the paralysis of hopelessness. You are dominated by a fear that if your try again you will once again fail. You can begin to settle that issue right now by returning to Romans 8 and meditating on verse 28 where it says, *"We know that in all things God works for the good of those who love him, who have been called according to his purpose."*

The verse from the classic hymn "How Firm a Foundation" expresses it this way, "When through fiery trials thy pathway shall lie, my grace all sufficient, shall be thy supply; the flames shall not hurt thee, I only design, thy dross to consume, and thy gold to refine."

1 Peter 1:6-7 says, "*In this you greatly rejoice, though now for a little while you may have had to suffer grief in all kinds of trials. These have come so that you faith of greater worth than gold, which perishes even though refined by fire, may be proved genuine and may result in praise, glory, and honor when Jesus Christ is revealed.*"

The time has come for us to stop whining over the things that did not work out the way we expected in the past and start winning in behalf of those who need the touch of the love of Christ flowing through us. We live in a hurting world which wants to see the light, love and hope of Christ shining in us.

Moses let his light shine in the midst of injustice. He confronted Pharaoh and things went from bad to worse. In fact the very people Moses was trying to help responded to his attempts in Exodus 5:21 by saying, "...*you have made us a stench to Pharaoh and his officials and have put a sword in their hand to kill us."*

Many at this point would have given up but not Moses. As he reached out to God, God responded five times in Exodus chapter 6 by saying, *"I am the Lord..."*

Maybe at this moment you are like Isaiah, feeling hopeless over the moral condition of our country. Then do what Isaiah did when he looked into the sky one day and *"...saw the Lord sitting on a throne, high and lifted up"* (Isaiah 6:1). When he did that his whole perspective changed.

It's a fact unless your eyes are fixed on the Lord Jesus as Hebrews 12:2 says, you will not be able to have hope when thing go from bad to worse. *"Let us fix our eyes on Jesus, the author and perfecter of our faith, who for the joy set before him endured the cross, scoring its shame and sat down at the right hand of the throne of God. Consider him who endured such opposition from sinful men, so that you will not grow weary and lose heart."*

As Moses looked to the living God, he was able to hear God also say in Exodus 6:7-8, *I will bring you out, I will take you as my own people, I will be your God, I will bring you to the promised land, I will give it to you as a possession.* But we read in Exodus 6:9 that "*Moses reported this to the Israelites but they did not listen to him because of their discouragement and cruel bondage.*" Even though he got this response, Moses did not give up and lose hope. He obeyed God and God worked through him.

In order to experience this touch of hope provided through the power and presence of the resurrected Christ, we must be set free from the most populated prison in the world. This is an oppressive prison that has more inmates than beds. In this prison the prisoners are hopelessly held captive by their wants. These are the prisoners who always want something bigger, faster, better, or different than what they have now.

If you feel better when you have more then you are in the Prison of Want. So many, year after year, miss the touch of Jesus because they remain captivated in the Prison of Want. This is the prison where satisfaction comes from some-thing you drink, drive, deposit, digest, devour or divulge yourself in.

If we want to be set free from this prison, then we must discover the key found in Psalm 23:1. There is says, *"The Lord is my Shephard; I shall not want."* Like the Psalmist David we must go to the pasture where contentment abides. It is in this pasture that we experience the freedom from always having to have more and more and more. It is there we develop hope along with a desire to touch Jesus.

Paul, having touched Jesus declared, *"I have learned to be satisfied with the things I have…I know how to live when I am poor and I know how to live when I have plenty"* (Philippians 4:11-12).

Jesus has come to set the captives of greed free by touching them with his love. For "…*godliness with contentment is great gain*" (1 Timothy 6:6). When one surrenders to Christ the doors to the Prison of Want are opened and the person is set free.

If we desire to touch God we must realize the hopelessness and fear can isolate us. It is through reconnecting with creation that we are also able to touch Jesus as our eyes are opened to our Creator's wonders. Come to the window and behold the wonders of His creation. Hear the chirping of the birds. Stop and watch the squirrels. Look at the sky and the floating clouds. **What variety there is in God's vast universe!** Allow His Spirit to enable you to reconnect, to deliver you from the asphalt jungle of hopelessness. Feel the earth beneath you and the breeze wrapping itself around you. Experience the life and hope that God has placed in His world.

When spring arrives plant something, and as you do experience a new connection with the life placed in that seed. Planting is an investment in the future. As a new cycle of life miraculously emerges, so will your connection with the Creator, as you rediscover that all life is a miracle filled with hope. Explore the sense of touch as you let the soil crumble within your hand. Smell the fragrance of the flowers. Thank God for the natural sounds which can take your mind from worrying and allow you to be reconnected with His loving presence.

Life is a gift. Learn to live it and love it as you are reconnected with the God of hope described in Romans 15:13. *"May the God of hope fill you with all joy and peace as you trust in him, so that you may overflow with hope by the power of the Holy Spirit."*

Today is the day to break through the crowd of negative thoughts and hopelessness. **Touch Jesus, the God of hope, and discover for yourself how He is the way, the truth and the life.** As scripture says and all of creation declares, Jesus is, *"...the image of the invisible God, the firstborn over all creation. For in him all things were created: things in heaven and on earth, visible and invisible, whether thrones or powers or rulers or authorities; all things have been created through him and for him. He is before all things, and in* *him all things hold together"* (Colossians 1:15-17).

    Touch Jesus now and experience His touch of Love and the hope it brings in this age of hopelessness. Through Him you will have life both now and for all eternity.

Learning to Touch Jesus Through the Exploration of the Scriptures

1. How does Mark 5:25, 26 describe the hopelessness of the woman who came to Jesus?

2. What did she do in her desperation?

3. What was Jesus' response?

4. How can you touch Jesus according to Matthew 25:31-46?

5. In what ways does Matthew 28:20 and Romans 8:37-39 give you hope?

6. According to 1 Peter 1:6-7 what good can come out of all kinds of trials?

7. What did Moses do to continue to have hope even when things seemed to go from bad to worse?

8. Explain the directives Hebrews 12:2 gives us in order that we may continue to have hope in times of difficulty?

9. How does the prison of want keep us from living a life of hope?

10. In what way does creation show us that life is a miracle filled with hope?

Singing The Songs of Hope Found in Revelation
Chapter 6

The Bible begins with a wonderful message of how God created the earth and all that lives upon it. It begins in a garden and in the last book of the Bible, Revelation, ends in a garden.

Creation and re-creation is the message that God gives us in His Holy Scriptures. It is this message that shows us that in spite of what the world may throw at us, because Christ is risen, the songs of hope can continue to flow from Revelation.

How I must strive to not let anything keep me from hearing the music of the garden. This means I must not only continue to hear all of creation praising God but I must join in that praise and worship. As I do this I am reminded in the depths of my being that "God is love" and that He has everything under control. *"Salvation and glory and power belong to our God, for true and just are His judgments"* (Revelation 19:1-2).

I am told over and over in the wonders of creation and in the Scripture, that **God has everything under control.** As I hear and participate in the music of the garden, this knowledge begins to move from my mind into my emotions and will power. As this happens I am free to join Paul as he declares, "*I can do all things through Christ who strengthens me*" (Philippians 4:13).

This strength through Christ can come forth in our lives as we choose to believe what God has spoken. That is what John did when he wrote the Book of Revelation. In this book the big question he asked was not, "How will the world end?" But, "Whom does the world belong?" John saw that the world under Rome's power was a place which competed for people's loyalties. John used a wide range of imagery to hold the reader's attention. This included the harlot that had an endless appetite for all the goods the world could produce.

Revelation takes its readers on a roller coaster ride from the heights of heaven in the presence of the Almighty, to an earth where the beast and its power wants to control all through brute force. I see in Revelation a direct challenge to the social and political forces that diminish the lives of not only the homeless but all human life.

On the one side I am getting a clearer picture of the political forces controlled by the gentrification of those who would fuel the economic interest of the developers. This is done with out of control tax abatements, stadiums, and the other pet projects of the elitists that shove the poor and homeless out of sight and out of mind.

The book of Revelation gives us hope that, in spite of the charges and the counter charges, the slain lamb will be victorious. This lamb, the sacrificial Christ, is contrasted with the beast who exercises its oppressive power through the police and the military. Such oppression involves the enforcement of the regulations of the rich and powerful even to the point of death. The lamb on the other hand wins victory through death and give the ultimate gift of life through its resurrection.

One of the most diabolical effects that the shutdown of 1411 Locust in St. Louis had on the homeless was the fact they were removed from a Spiritual House of Hope that did more than provide food and shelter. The daily Bible Studies, prayer meetings, worship services and supportive community of believers gave the homeless the hope and faith they needed daily to face what could seem as impossible obstacles. But this didn't cause the staff at New Life Evangelistic Center to give up. When they were locked out of 1411 Locust they then took the message of the resurrection to the streets sharing that there is hope because Christ is risen.

Those marching to the different drum beat provided by the Resurrected Christ, are given hope even in those moments when the beast seems to be in total control and all hell is breaking out.

Suddenly with the accompaniment of music, the scene shifts from one of hopeless-ness to one of hope both now and for all eternity. I find this hope kept alive by not only the scenes of hope expressed in Revelation but the music that has resulted from the inspiration Revelation provides.

This hope is generated through the music of Handel's "Messiah" and the "Battle Hymn of the Republic." Both of these works, although vastly different from each other, were inspired by the Book of Revelation. In God's battle for justice for believers, the truth is that all human life is valuable. It is this truth that we believe will ultimately carry the day.

Affliction was a way of life for Sojourner Truth, but she refused to let it define her future or enslave her in hopelessness. Sojourner Truth found the hope she needed to be the first African American woman to win a case in a white man's court. She drew her hope and strength from a hymn centered on Revelation's New Jerusalem. The song of the New Jerusalem showed her a light-filled future in which even the marginalized at the bottom of the social ladder will someday wear the royal robes that give people dignity. For her and hundreds like her, who have sung this song of hope, it gives the incentive needed to persevere in the present.

"Slave Songs of the United States," which was published in 1867 reveals the songs that slaves made up in their prayer meetings to keep hope alive. One of the spirituals that draws on the scene of the New Jerusalem is called, "Blow Your Trumpet Gabriel." It begins, "The tallest tree in Paradise, the Christians call the tree of life. And I hope that trumpet might blow me home to the New Jerusalem." The singer wants Gabriel to change things for the better with the blast of his horn and, "blow me home to the New Jerusalem." The hope is that the singer will be taken from this life in the present into that mansion that Jesus promised he would prepare for His faithful.

The spiritual, "My Father, How Long?" was considered by the slave owners as being subversive. The song started out innocently enough, "My Father, how long, My Father how long, My Father how long, this poor sinner suffer here." The response gave words of hope that it won't be long that they must suffer here. The verses following speak of the Lord calling the singers home, so they can walk the golden streets of the New Jerusalem.

It was when the song concludes, "we will soon be free" and in the final verse, "We'll fight for liberty, when the Lord will call us home" that most concerned the slave owners as it blurs the line between the future and the present. This hope for the next world gave incentive to bring change in this world.

It is this hope that fueled the staff of New Life Evangelistic Center to double their efforts to be "hope dealers" on the street once 1411 Locust was closed. It involved not only expanding present NLEC programs but involved a team daily providing hope to those who were homeless. New Life became the number one provider of transportation for the homeless with the distribution of over 1,000 bus tickets weekly. In addition, Safe Houses were opened for the homeless women and children as the training programs were expanded for the homeless men.

With each day that passes I know that growing numbers of men, women and children are suffering as they try to survive outdoors. Yet, I also know that getting bitter over this injustice will not solve anything. **I must choose to let the songs of praise and hope that Christ provides flow from me each and every day.**

In order to help me do that I have to remember the words of Archbishop Oscar Romeo who said prior to his death by an assassin's bullet, "Don't be led astray either by the allure of power and money or by following the false ideologies. True hope is not found there either. True hope is not found in a revolution of violence and bloodshed, and hope is not found in money and power – neither on the left nor on the right. The hope that we must account for and that makes us speak with valor is found in Christ, who reigns after death, even after murderous death. And with Him reign all who have preached His justice, His hope, and his peace."

With this fact in mind, I know we can keep hope alive, even as we go through the fires of injustice. In order to keep hope alive we must abide daily in the love and power of the resurrected Christ. It won't be long and we will hear a loud voice from the throne saying, *"Look! God's dwelling place is now among the people, and he will dwell with them. They will be his people, and God himself will be with them and be their God. 'He will wipe every tear from their eyes. There will be no more death or mourning or crying or pain, for the old order of things has passed away,' He who was seated on the throne said, "I am making everything new!"* (Revelation 21:3-5).

A new day is dawning. We must keep the faith and have hope. Faith is choosing to boldly believe and receive the hope God records in His Book of Hope, the Bible. This hope is the result of faith which releases the creative power of God's word.

The creative power of scriptures give us the strength to boldly proclaim *"I can do all things through Christ who strengthens me*" (Philippians 4:13). We can then begin each day with a song in our heart declaring it is Magnificent Monday. Hope for a great Tuesday allows us to sing it is a Terrific Tuesday. Regardless of what day it may be we can sing forth with the birds it a Wonderful Wednesday – a Thankful Thursday – Freedom Friday – Satisfied Saturday or Sanctified Sunday.

Every day becomes a gift of hope from God where we sing, "*Give thanks to the Lord, for He is good: For His loving kindness is everlasting*" (Psalm 118:1).

Experiencing Strength from Songs of Hope

1. How does the Resurrected Christ allow us to sing songs of hope with the rest of creation?

2. Where does Revelation give a direct challenge to the ungodly social and political forces?

3. In what ways has the book of Revelation inspired songs of hope and freedom for the oppressed?

4. What are some of the songs that have come from Revelation to give hope?

5. How can these songs inspire hope within us today?

6. Where did Archbishop Oscar Romeo say true hope could be found?

7. According to Revelation 21:3-5 what must we do to keep hope alive?

8. In what ways does faith produce songs of hope which releases the creative power of God's word?

9. How can we begin each day with a song of hope?

10. In what way does praising God release a song of hope in our lives?

Celebrating with Songs of Hope
Chapter 7

Are you experiencing the dark night of the soul? Does everything seem hopeless, senseless, and useless no matter how hard you try? Perhaps, like Job, you are crying out, "*Where is God my Maker, Who gives songs in the night?*" (Job 35:10).

Charles Spurgeon stated, "Many a night do we have—nights of sorrow, nights of persecution, nights of doubt, nights of bewilderment, nights of anxiety, nights of oppression, nights of ignorance – nights of all kinds, which possess our spirits and terrify our souls. But blessed be God, the Christian can say, '*My God gives me songs in the night.*'"

It is because, "*God so loved the world that He gave His one and only Son,*" that we can sing the songs of hope on the coldest, loneliest nights that life may throw at us. Not only does God proclaim, "*I have loved you with an everlasting love*" (Jeremiah 31:3), but He also demonstrated it through sending His Son, Jesus Christ, into the world.

Jesus, through His death on the cross, personally revealed the truth of John 15:13: *"Greater love has no one than this, that he lay down his life for his friends."* In Revelation 1:5-6 we see Jesus described as the One, *"Who loves us and has freed us from our sins by His blood, and has made us to be a kingdom and priests to serve His God and Father."*

Why is it so hard for us to receive the songs of hope in the midst of the nights of disappointment, tragedy and despair? These songs of hope are actually the proclamation of God's love revealed through the Scripture. They can also be heard in the millions of songs coming from creation and the presence of the Holy Spirit. That same Spirit of God, which from the beginning of time hovers over the waters of emptiness, formlessness and darkness, desires to bring forth order, music and light (see Genesis 1:1-4) in our lives.

These songs in the night include that of the angel to the shepherds when the angel declared, *"Do not be afraid. I bring you good news of great joy that will be for all the people"* (Luke 2:10). This command to not fear in the midst of the darkness of uncertainty is based upon the fact that, *"He brought you and me to the banqueting house, and His banner over us is love"* (Song of Solomon 2:4).

We are told explicitly in Romans 8:37-39 that nothing can separate us from the love of God. *"No, in all these things we are more than conquerors through Him who loved us. For I am convinced that neither death nor life, neither angels nor demons, neither the present nor the future, nor any powers, neither height nor depth, nor anything else in all creation, will be able to separate us from the love of God that is in Christ Jesus our Lord."*

We all go through that dark night of the soul. At such a time it is critical that we **hear God's songs of hope and know He will deliver us.**

Paul shares in 2 Corinthians 1:8-10, how difficult times cause us to rely on God. *"For we do not want you to be unaware, brothers, of the affliction we experienced in Asia. For we were so utterly burdened beyond our strength that we despaired of life itself. Indeed, we felt that we had received the sentence of death. But that was to make us rely not on ourselves but on God who raises the dead. He delivered us from such a deadly peril, and He will deliver us. On Him we have to set our hope that He will deliver us again."*

During these difficult times we must not give up. Remember from them we learn not to trust in ourselves but the Living God who raises the dead. Because Christ is Risen we can have hope both now and for all eternity.

As we go forth in obedience sharing God's songs of hope, we must not fail to see the need for justice. Developers and special interest groups are raping and robbing the land. Babies are being aborted. The poor are given legal lynching in the name of the death penalty. The oil industry has bought off the politicians. People are psychologically enslaved to believe they cannot survive unless they are on the electric grid depending on the big utility companies. The homes of the poor are being condemned and the homeless are being driven out of the downtown areas. The time has come for the people of God to arise with their songs of justice and direct actions providing hope and help in this time of darkness.

Songs of joy, consisting of just words, are meaningless as the actual human conditions and moral issues are ignored. God responds by saying, *"They have become a burden to me; I am weary of hearing them. When you spread out your hands in prayer, I will hide my eyes from you; even if you offer many prayers, I will not listen. Your hands are full of blood; wash and make yourselves clean. Take your evil deeds out of my sight!"* (Isaiah 1:14-16).

Making it harder for the poor to get health care, creating laws which further victimize the most vulnerable in society, to these and other oppressive conditions the prophet Isaiah declares, *"Woe to those who make unjust laws, to those who issue oppressive decrees, to deprive the poor of their rights and withhold justice from the oppressed of my people, making widows their prey and robbing the fatherless"* (Isaiah 10:1-2).

It is not enough to sing songs of hope and live in a land that claims to be founded on equality and justice. Each follower of Christ must work to see that the poor and powerless have their rights. When people are oppressed, it is difficult for them to praise God and worship Him in spirit and in truth.

As believers it is necessary that we not only listen to the songs of love and hope that God shares with us in the darkness of life but also that we share them with others who are going through difficult times. Jesus declares, *"I tell you the truth, whatever you did for one of the least of these brothers (and sisters) of Mine, you did for Me"* (Matthew 25:40).

Now let us celebrate with songs of hope in word and deed. The water of life, Jesus, is creating new life. At the wedding in Cana He illustrates this by turning water into wine using 6 stone water jars. These represent the 6 days of creation (John 2:1-11).

A new creation is taking place. Almost every miracle Jesus did was renewal of a fallen creation. He is creating new wine (life) through the restoring of sight, making the lame walk, even raising the dead.

Maybe you are one of those who have spent most of your life drinking the cheap wine of a self-centered life. Now you find yourself living in darkness and hopelessness. Come now to the living waters of life, Jesus Christ, and let Him give you the new wine of His Spirit and the new life resulting from His resurrection. Discover what it means to experience God's songs of hope in the darkness of night.

If you accepted the reality that there is hope because Christ if risen then sing out your songs of hope with direct help. God has placed you in this time and place at this historical moment.

If you are experiencing hope fatigue then take up the double-edged sword of praise. *"May the praise of God be in their mouths and a double-edged sword in their hands"* (Psalm 149:6). It is the Word of God, which is that double-edged sword (Hebrews 4:12) and the power of singing forth the songs of praise in the darkest of hopelessness that will sustain and strengthen you.

In the Scriptures we are reminded of God's eternal love for us. This is a love that will encourage us in the darkest of nights. *"I remember my affliction and my wandering, the bitterness and the gall. I will remember them, and my soul is downcast within me. Yet this I call to mind and therefore I have hope: Because of the Lord's great love we are not consumed, for His compassions never fail. They are new every morning; great is your faithfulness"* (Lamentations 3:19-23).

We will truly be strengthened and cheered up as we sing of God's faithfulness. **There is nothing like singing to keep your spirit alive.** It will also encourage others around you who would otherwise be adversely affected by your negative attitude.

Remember, as you hear or sing uplifting songs, you will keep your heart full of praise. Then your mind will be filled with desires to help others who are going through the dark valley of hopelessness.

Now is the time for each of us to sing forth the songs of victory provided through our Resurrected Lord and Savior Jesus Christ. After all, *"We are more than conquerors through Him (our Lord Jesus) who loved us. For I am convinced that neither death, nor life, neither angels, nor demons, neither the present, nor the future, nor any powers, neither height, nor depth, nor anything else in all creation, will be able to separate us from the love of God that is in Christ Jesus our Lord"* (Romans 8:37-39).

The next time you feel hopeless and afraid, look at life from Jesus' perspective. Then believe Him as He says to you, *"Don't be afraid; just believe"* (Mark 5:36).

Singing songs of hope or listening to music glorifying God awakens you to Christ's presence in the midst of the storms of life. He told His disciples as they panicked in the middle of the lake during a storm, *"'Take courage! It is I. Don't be afraid,' Then He climbed in the boat with them, and the wind died down"* (Mark 6:50-51).

Let Jesus come into *"the boat"* of your life and rest in the reality of His everlasting love for you (Jeremiah 31:3). *"Bring every thought captive unto Christ"* (2 Corinthians 10:5). Ask the Holy Spirit to make Scripture come alive to you so that you can visualize God speaking to you in each passage and every biblical narrative. As you do this you will begin to celebrate life with God's songs of hope.

Please answer the following to help you allow songs of hope spring forth.

1. How is it possible for us to sing songs of hope in nights of anxiety, doubts and sorrow?

2. What hope did the songs of the angels bring the shepherds in Luke 2:10?

3. What reason is given in 2 Corinthians 1:8-10 as to why we would encounter hopeless and despairing situations?

4. Why is it critical that we provide help to the oppressed in order that they may experience hope?

5. How does the new life Jesus provides give us hope both now and for all eternity?

6. In what ways does listening to uplifting Christian music and singing songs of praise give us hope?

7. What does Lamentations 3:19-23 say we need to call to mind to have hope?

8. What reason does Romans 8:37-39 give us for singing songs of hope even when we are facing overwhelming problems?

9. What is Jesus telling us in Mark 5:36?

10. How does singing songs of hope and listening to Christian music help you bring every thought captive according to 2 Corinthians 10:5?

Living in Hope
Chapter 8

God has called all of us to live in hope and share hope with a world drowning in hopelessness. Psalm 27:14 tells us to *"Wait and hope for and expect the Lord; be brave and of good courage and let your heart be stout and enduring. Yes, wait for and hope for and expect the Lord."*

It may seem hard to wait, but we can wait and have hope knowing that God's delay is not God's denial. Without hope, which is the oxygen for our souls we will give in to despair, hopeless-ness and depression. When there is no hope, we will feel that life is suffocating us with one endless problem after another.

As Hope Dealers we can offer direct help to the hurting and homeless. *"For the needy shall not always be forgotten, and the <u>hope</u> of the meek and the poor shall not perish forever"* (Psalm 9:18). Knowing this we will in these last days take our eyes off inflation and our own problems and become dealers of hope as we directly help those in need.

We are able to respond to the needs of the poor and elderly because as we live in hope, we will declare to the Lord, "*You are my hiding place and my shield; I hope in Your word*" (Psalm 119:114).

The word of God, commonly referred to as the Bible, could also be called the book of hope. In it we find the promises, power and presence of God affirmed over and over. We are told to, "...*trust in the Lord (commit yourself to Him, lean on Him, hope confidently in Him) forever; for the Lord God is an everlasting Rock (the Rock of Ages)*" (Isaiah 26:4).

To trust in the Lord means to have faith in God. Faith is the substance of hope. As Hebrews 11:1 says, "...*faith is the assurance of things hoped for.*" Without faith Hebrews 11:6 also says it is impossible to please God. It is faith in God which gives us the strength to be there with direct help when people are hurting.

We will live in hope as we daily immerse ourselves in scriptures like Jeremiah 20:11 where it says, *"For I know the thoughts and plans that I have for you, says the Lord, thoughts and plans for welfare and peace and not for evil, to give you <u>hope</u> and a future."*

In order to live in hope, we must grasp the reality that Ephesians 1:18 speaks of, *"Having the eyes of your heart flooded with light, so that you can know and understand the <u>hope</u> to which He has called you, and how rich His glorious inheritance is in the saints."*

We have a living hope. As 1 Peter 1:3 says, *"Blessed be the God and Father of our Lord Jesus Christ! According to His great mercy, He has caused us to be born again to a living <u>hope</u> through the resurrection of Jesus Christ from the dead."*

There is hope for Christ is Risen. Now we need to learn how to rest in this hope during this age of anxiety. *"(Resting) in the <u>hope</u> of eternal life, (life) which the ever truthful God who cannot deceive,* *promised before the world or the ages to time began"* (Titus 1:2).

Paul, knowing that putting our minds on the reality of salvation is essential for resting in this hope, refers to this as putting on the helmet of the hope of salvation in 1 Thessalonians 5:8: *"Let us be sober having put on the breastplate of faith and love, and for a helmet the <u>hope</u> of salvation."* We have this hope of salvation because Jesus Christ paid the price for our sins by dying on the cross. His resurrection following this death clearly shows that as we trust in Him we will be saved. *"...who through Him are believers in God, who raised Him from the dead and gave Him glory, so that your faith and <u>hope</u> are in God"* (1 Peter 1:21).

There are many who claim to have their faith and hope in God but yet their lives reflect hopelessness, despair, and frustration. The problem is God's message of hope is blocked by misplaced faith that believes hope can only spring forth from monetary wealth. Such misunderstanding provides the seed bed for hopelessness. This is the result of not understanding that

<u>hope doesn't involve getting rich but living richly</u>. Such rich living is a result of faith which is the substance of hope planted deep within which, in turn, provides an anchor for our souls even as we journey through the storms of life. *"We have this <u>hope</u> as an anchor for the soul"* (Hebrews 6:19).

In order to secure such an anchor we must ask God to help us develop an attitude of gratitude for all that has been given to us, rather than constantly desiring more and more. This means placing our hope and faith in God and not in money. Such hope involves self-control and working to place our minds on the hope God provided through His love and not the three thousand marketing messages that we are bombarded with each day. As 1 Peter 1:13 says, *"Therefore, prepare your minds for action, and being sober-minded, set your <u>hope</u> fully on the grace that will be brought to you at the revelation of Jesus Christ."*

Setting our hope fully on the grace of Jesus Christ is possible only as we *"flee idols"* as Paul told us in 1 Corinthians 10:14.

If we have our hope in the idols of this world, it won't be long and these idols will soon rob us of all hope.

When Jesus told the rich ruler in Mark 10:17-31 and Luke 18:18-30 to sell all and give it to the poor, Jesus was challenging the man to transfer his hope based on his wealth to God the Giver and Source of all life. The man "...*went sadly away because he had many possessions*" (Mark 10:22). He was possessed by his possessions. "*As for the rich in this world, charge them not to be proud and arrogant and contemptuous of others, nor to set their hope on uncertain riches, but on God. Who richly and ceaselessly provides us with everything for (our) enjoyment*" (1 Timothy 6:17).

Those walking in the darkness of hopelessness see only despair and loneliness. The miracles of creation can be taking place all around them, but they do not recognize them as such. Everything is formless, empty and filled with the darkness of discouragement and negativism. In Genesis 1:2-3 we read, "*...now the earth was formless and empty, darkness was *over the surface of the deep, and the Spirit of God was hovering over the waters. And God said, 'Let there be light,' and there was light."* For there to be light, hope and order in our lives, we need the Spirit of God to hover over our troubled waters of hopelessness. Then we need the Word of God to proclaim light and hope in the midst of this dark hopeless situation.

If we are going to live in hope, we need Jesus, the Word of Life, to remove the darkness of sin from us and bring forth the light of His forgiveness. In order for this to happen, we must respond to the movement of the Spirit and repent of our sins and declare in word and deed "Now I Surrender to You, O Lord." **This surrender means that we give God our actions, our words and all that we are and own.** In order for all things to be brought into full harmony with His divine order of creation we must let go of our own habitually disordered fear, along with our runaway passions, desires and emotions.

I realize that as we live this new life in Christ, and express hope in the midst of hopelessness, many in the world will consider us foolish or even crazy. Leonard Sweet, in his book <u>Jesus Drives Me Crazy</u>, uses the word "nuts" as an acronym for **Never Underestimate The Spirit**. "Let the unbelievers consider us nuts! We have learned to never underestimate the Spirit. As the Holy Spirit works in our lives, we learn that the more status that Jesus has in our lives, the more we find ourselves confronting the status quo. The more Jesus becomes the Prince of Peace, the more we recognize the social injustices and frequently disturb the peace of the rich and powerful".

As we allow the Holy Spirit to hover over our troubled waters and let the Hope and Love of Christ enter the dark area of our lives, we will learn to never underestimate the power of the Spirit. God's miracle power at work in our lives will allow us to not only experience hope but share it with everyone we meet.

Sometimes we feel like Frodo in the Lord of the Rings, who said he wished the master ring had not been found in his lifetime. "So do I," said Gandalf, "and so do all who live to see such times. But that is not for them to decide. All we have to decide is what to do with the time that is given us."

You and I must also decide. Are we going to live in the light, hope and harmony of creation or are we going to live in the darkness and hopelessness that our culture of death serves up daily. *"This is the verdict: Light has come into the world, but men loved darkness instead of light, because their deeds were evil. Everyone who does evil hates the light, and will not come into the light for fear that his deeds will be exposed. But whoever lives by the truth comes into the light, so that it may be seen plainly that what he has done has been done through God"* (The words of Jesus Christ found in John 3:19-21).

When everyone else is living in hopeless-ness and darkness, the one living in the light and hope of Christ will be considered by the world as being nuts. But if being considered nuts means never underestimating the Spirit, who cares what others think?

We are able, through the grace of God manifested through Jesus Christ, to live in hope because we know that "...*the effectual fervent prayer of a righteous man (and woman) availeth much*" (James 5:16).

Joshua prayed and the sun stood still. Nineveh's inhabitants prayed and God reversed His death sentence upon them. Hezekiah prayed and God let him live fifteen years longer. Samson prayed and God restored his lost power. Joseph prayed in prison, was given an interpretation to Pharaoh's dream, was made second in command of Egypt and saved his family from starvation. Daniel prayed and God shut the lion's mouth. Elisha, Peter and Paul prayed and the dead were raised to life.

As you move from darkness and hopelessness into light and life, you will discover you are *"... more than a conqueror through Him (Jesus) who loves us"* (Romans 8:38). After all, Jesus said in John 12:46, "*I have come into the world as a light, so that no one who believes in me should stay in darkness."* As the late Adrian Rogers said, "Never doubt in the dark what God has shown you in the light."

As we remain in the light, love, and presence of Jesus Christ daily, He promises, *"If you remain in Me and my Words remain in you, ask whatever you wish, and it will be given you"* (John 15:7). That is God's promise to us at this hour spoken through Jesus who said, *"If you believe, you will receive whatever you ask for in prayer"* (Matthew 21:22).

We can have hope at this time of hopelessness because, *"This hope does not disappoint us, because God has poured out His love into our hearts by the Holy Spirit, whom He has given us"* (Romans 5:5).

It's a fact hope centered in God and His promise is hope that endures. He will meet all of our needs as reflected in Psalm 25:3, 20-21. The reason this hope does not disappoint is that God has poured out His love into our hearts (1 John 4:8,16). This love of God poured out into our hearts provides hope in the most difficult and seemingly impossible situations because we know that God is love.

God is not only our Eternal Hope Dealer, but Healer, Deliverer, Savior, Comforter, Provider and Sustainer. What a mighty God we serve!

Even the trials, tribulations and afflictions we suffer on a day-by-day basis can serve to build character and hope within us as we look to our Risen Savior. *"For our light, momentary affliction (this slight distress of the passing hour) is ever more and more abundantly preparing and producing and achieving for us an everlasting weight of glory (beyond all measure, excessively surpassing all comparisons and all calculations, a vast and transcendent glory and blessedness never to cease). Since we consider and look not to the things that are seen but to the things that are unseen; for the things that are visible are temporal (brief and fleeting), but the things that are invisible are deathless and everlasting"* (2 Corinthians 4:17-18).

Glory be to God! Because of His infinite love, mercy and grace we are people who can live in hope both now and for all eternity. Look at how Romans 15:13, calls Him the God of hope as it declares, *"May the God of hope fill you with all joy and peace as you trust in Him so that you may overflow with hope by the power of the Holy Spirit."*

The key to experiencing all joy and peace is to trust in the God of hope. As you trust in Him remember you will overflow with hope by the power of the Holy Spirit.

Hope involves faith. *"For in this hope we were saved. But hope that is seen is no hope at all. Who hopes for what he already has?"* (Romans 8:24).

Hope is the oxygen for your soul. Continue to trust in the God of hope and let His hope flow into the essence of your being at this moment. Be a Hope Dealer sharing this hope with everyone you know. As you do this you will see Him do exceedingly far beyond what you can ask or think.

Remember at every moment no matter what life may throw at you, there is hope, for Christ is Risen. Live in the reality of this hope and discover the joy of overflowing with hope as you become a Hope Dealer for the glory of God.

Learning from the Scriptures
How to Live in Hope

1. What is the reason you can have hope no matter what the circumstances might be?

2. How can we trust and hope in the Lord according to Isaiah 26:4?

3. In what way can we rest in the fact Christ is risen according to Titus 1:2?

4. How can it be said that hope doesn't involve getting rich but living richly?

5. When it comes to experiencing hope why should we Never Underestimate the Spirit?

6. In John 3:19-21 Jesus says, "...*whoever lives by the truth comes into the truth.*" How does experiencing this light help us have hope?

7. How did hope produce prayer that changed things for Joshua, Hezekiah, Samson, Joseph, Daniel and Elisha?

8. What does our momentary affliction produce?

9. Romans 15:13 calls God a God of hope. What does this passage ask that God would do in our life?

10. What does Romans 8:24 mean when it says, "...*hope that is seen is not hope at all*"?

Maintaining Hope In Spite of the Circumstances
Chapter 9

A father who loves, a father who cares, this is the heartfelt desire of any child. Tragically that is not often the case. So many having been denied the love of a father are now living with the ghosts of rejection and neglect from the past. As a result bitterness poisons present relationships until loneliness and hopelessness become their only companions.

We are now given the opportunity to shake off the chains of bitterness and loneliness that enslave us by accepting the reality that we have a loving Heavenly Father. This reality is written across the skies every morning as the sun rises and is also broadcast in all the sounds of creation which praise God throughout the day.

Over fifty-two years ago I was awakened to the point I was able to begin to rejoice in the hope provided by the love of my Heavenly Father. Under His direction

I began a journey down the road of life in which I gained a deeper under-standing of who my Heavenly Father is and what He desires from His children.

Proverbs 20:24 asks a question concerning the road of life and then immediately answers it when it declares, *"How can we understand the road we travel? It is the Lord who directs our steps."*

At the young age of twenty-three, the Lord, my Heavenly Father directed my steps to start the New Life Evangelistic Center. **Each day required a new step of faith.** The problem was it wasn't the steps I wanted to take, it was the elevator. I wanted to get right to the top.

Things were great when God in His mercy would answer prayer after prayer. As that happened I couldn't help but rejoice in the Lord. Then to prevent me from becoming a spoiled spiritual brat my Heavenly Father started saying no. He wanted to teach me that while I was trying to build a ministry He was trying to build a man. The only way I could grow as a man of God was to be put in one trial and tribulation after another that would exercise my faith muscle and cause me to trust my Heavenly Father to provide.

These trials and tribulations often included people I depended on who would suddenly desert me when I needed them most. Financial needs would mount. At times I felt God was taking me out to his woodshed and giving me one spiritual spanking after another. As I was disciplined I was told in Hebrew 12:5-12, *"My child, don't ignore it when the Lord disciplines you, and don't be discouraged when He corrects you. For the Lord disciplines those He loves, and punishes those He accepts as His children. As you endure this divine discipline, remember that God is treating you as His own children."*

"Whoever heard of a child who was never disciplined? If God doesn't discipline you as He does all His children, it means that you are illegitimate and are not really His children after all. Since we respect our earthly fathers who disciplined us, should we not all the more cheerfully submit to the

discipline of our Heavenly Father and live forever?"

"For our earthly fathers disciplined us for a few years, doing the best they know how. But God's discipline is always right and good for us because it means that we will share in His Holiness. No discipline is enjoyable while it is happening – it is painful! But afterward there will be a quiet harvest of right living for those who are trained in this way."

"So take a new grip with your tired hands and stand firm on your shaky legs. Mark out a straight path for your feet. Then those who follow you, though they are weak and lame, will not stumble and fall but will become strong."

When you come into the realization that your Heavenly Father has ordered the steps you will take down the road of life you will see that setbacks and disappointments are not the end but only the beginning of a deeper walk with Him. That is why David would say in the 23rd Psalm, "Yea though I walk through the valley of the shadow of *death I will fear no evil."* David knew that he did not have to fear because his Heavenly Father was with him.

We have a Heavenly Father who is all powerful, all knowing and present everywhere. Psalm 37:23-25 tells us that, *"...the steps of the godly are directed by the Lord, He delights in every detail of their lives. Though they stumble they will not fall, for the Lord holds them by the hand. Once I was young, and now I am old. Yet I have never seen the godly forsaken, nor seen their children begging for bread."*

What a wonderful Heavenly Father we have. With each passing day as I get older I can testify of the Father's goodness and faithfulness. I think of those earlier years at New Life when we would literally gather around the dinner table which had no food on it and pray. The doorbell would ring and upon running downstairs we would open the door and discover bags of food. Only heaven knows how many time the Father has sent forth His angels to gather the monies needed to pay the bills and provide our daily food and meet other needs.

In Isaiah 40:25-31 we are reminded what an all-powerful Heavenly Father we have when He asks, *"To whom will you compare me? Who is my equal? Look up into the heavens. Who created the stars? He brings them out one after another, calling each by name. And He counts them to see that none are lost or have strayed away. How can you say God refuses to hear your case? Have you never heard or understood? Don't you know that the Lord is the everlasting God, the Creator of all the earth? He never grows faint or weary! No one can measure the depths of His understanding. He gives power to those who are tired and worn out; He offers strength to the weak. Even youths will become exhausted and young men will give up. But those who wait on the Lord will find new strength. They will fly on wings like eagles. They will run and not grow weary. They will walk and not faint."*

Our Heavenly Father loves each and every one of us and gives us the power we need to be more than conquerors through Christ who strengthens us. He sent His Son, our Brother, Redeemer and Savior, to die in our behalf in order that we may inherit the gift of eternal life. That ultimate rescue operation is described in John 3:16 *"For God, our Father, so loved the world that He sent His only begotten Son that whoever believes in Him shall not perish but have eternal life."*

It's impossible for us to claim that God is our Heavenly Father and at the same time hate God's children who may be of a different nationality or race. Some political candidates are trying to turn us away from our Heavenly Father and get us to fear those who are different until we accept their policies of hate and bigotry.

To those politicians who want us to separate from anyone who might be different and say we need to have more guns to protect ourselves Jesus would say, *"Love your enemies! Pray for those who persecute you! In that way, you will be acting as true children of your Father in Heaven"* (Matthew 5:44-45).

In Matthew 5 verses 13 and 14 Jesus says that as children of God we are the *"...salt of the earth"* and the *"...light of the world."* Then in verse 16 He declares, *"Let your good deeds shine out for all to see, so that everyone will praise your Heavenly Father."*

In Matthew 6 we are told to pray and not worry because *"...your heavenly Father already knows all your needs and He will give you all you need from day to day if you live for Him and make the kingdom of God your primary concern"* (Matthew 6:32-33).

It is Jesus' death and resurrection which makes it possible for us to have hope as we come into the presence of our Heavenly Father. That is why Jesus said in John 14:6, *"I am the way, the truth and the life. No one can come to the Father except through me."* In verses 10 and 11, Jesus further explains when He says, *"The words I say are not my own, but my Father who lives in me does His work through me. Just believe I am in the Father and the Father is in me."* Then Jesus goes on in verses 12-

14 and tells us the potential that exists in each of us if we will but believe in Him and let our Heavenly Father work through us. He declares, *"The truth is, anyone who believes in me will do the same works I have done, and even greater works, because I am going to be with the Father. You can ask for anything in my name, and I will do it, because the work of the Son brings glory to the Father. Yes, ask anything in my name, and I will do it."*

Jesus is making it very clear that if we are going to have a relationship with our Heavenly Father we must communicate with Him. This communication is commonly referred to as prayer.

The disciples, after observing Jesus' deep communication with the Father, asked Him to teach them how to pray. In Luke 11:2-4 and Matthew 6:9-13 Jesus teaches them what is commonly referred to as the Lord's Prayer. There we see Jesus beginning that prayer by saying, *"Our Father who art in heaven."* He didn't just say my Father. He said *"Our Father."* This means that God desires to be the Heavenly Father of each and every one of us.

In this great lesson on talking or praying to our Heavenly Father it should be noted that Jesus desired to see the Father glorified, and His will done on earth as it is in heaven. We can't really pray with power and see our needs met until we put first the Kingdom of God and His will for our lives.

Once we have it firmly established in our hearts and minds that our Heavenly Father is the supreme ruler of the universe and it is His Kingdom we want to see come forth, we are free to ask for the provision of our needs. This includes our daily bread or food, the forgiveness of sins, and deliverance from the evil one.

As I look back over the past fifty-two years I can think of a multitude of miracles that my Heavenly Father brought forth to meet what seemed like then impossible needs. In order to witness the miraculous out there I first had to see victory inside my own life. This meant a surrender in my heart, mind and spirit to the will of my

Heavenly Father and a desire to see His Kingdom come forth rather than my own. This surrender to the will of God allowed me to experience a peace that passes all understanding.

Jesus through His death and resurrection makes it possible for us as sinful human beings to not only have hope with God but to become His adopted children. For that reason Paul begins his letters in the New Testament by saying, "*May God our Father and the Lord Jesus Christ give you His grace and peace.*" Paul then goes on and prays in Ephesians 1:17 "*...that you may walk worthy of the Lord, fully increasing in the knowledge of God,*" our Heavenly Father.

Now I join Paul in praying that we "*...may walk worthy of the Lord (our Heavenly Father) fully pleasing Him, being fruitful in every good work and increasing in the knowledge of God.*" Jesus tells you what to do in Matthew 7:7-11 if you feel hopeless and your prayers to your Heavenly Father are not being answered, "*Keep on asking, and you will receive what *you ask for. Keep on seeking, and you will find. Keep on knocking, and the door will be opened to you. For everyone who asks, receives. Everyone who seeks, finds. And to everyone who knock, the door will be opened."*

"You parents—if your children ask for a loaf of bread, do you give them a stone instead? Or if they ask for a fish, do you give them as snake? Of course not! So if you sinful people know how to give good gifts to your children, how much more will your heavenly Father give good gifts to those who ask him."

As you study the scriptures you will discover how your Heavenly Father desires to not only give you good gifts but the greatest gift of all – eternal life through His Son, our Lord Jesus Christ. 1 John 3:1 says, *"See how great a love the Father has bestowed on us that we would be called children of God."*

Stop and think about what it means to be a child of the creator, sustainer and redeemer of heaven and earth. Scripture tells us "...*that as many as call the name of the Lord shall be called the Children of God*" (John 1:12).

Call upon Jesus Christ now. He is "...*the way, the truth and the life and no one comes to the Father except through Him*" (John 14:6). If you have truly repented of your sins and are trusting Jesus to save you, stop worrying so much and rejoice in the hope that He proclaims when He says, "*In my Father's house are many dwelling places; if it were not so, I would have told you; for I go to prepare a place for you*" (John 14:2).

Please answer the following questions to gain future insight into maintaining hope.

1. Why would God say no to some of our prayers?

2. What does Hebrews 12:5-12 tell us about discipline?

3. How does this help us to get a deeper understanding of why we can still be hopeful even when things don't go the way we expected?

4. Please list the three reasons Psalm 37:23-25 gives why we can remain hopeful even if we stumble?

5. Who does Matthew 5:13-14 say we are?

6. If we believe in Jesus what is possible according to John 14:12-14?

7. How does the Lord's Prayer give us hope that God wants to be our Heavenly Father?

8. Why is it so important to put first the Kingdom of God if we hope to get our prayers answered?

9. What does Jesus tell us to do in Matthew 7:7-11 if we feel hopeless and it doesn't seem our prayers are being answered?

10. How does 1 John 3:1, John 1:12 and John 14:2 all describe the great love Christ Jesus and God the Father has for us?

Receive God's Gift of Hope Through Faith and Prayer
Chapter 10

You may have lost everything, but you can start all over if you do not lose hope. We are told in Isaiah 43:18-19, *"Forget what happened! Don't think about the past. I am creating something new. There it is! Do you see it? I have put roads in deserts, streams in thirsty lands."*

So many are now depressed because the pain of the past and the unmet expectations of the present have removed all real hope for a miracle in their life. As a result, all they can think about is how they are going to exist in the present situation they are in which appears hopeless with no real future. The problem in just leaving our present circumstances provides no real solution, for the key is learning how to live with a hope that brings forth miracles. Dr. Charles R. Ringma has stated, "If we live in hope, we have a future. If hope dies, then the future dies with it. The person who is without hope can only live with the legacy of the past and the circumstances of the present."

I know from personal experience that as I live with hope I must bring "...*into captivity every thought to the obedience of Christ*" (2 Corinthians 10:5). Only then can I experience a hope that brings forth miracles.

As I strive to live with the hope in Christ that brings forth miracles I am awakened to the miracles of God's creation that "...*the world's a huge stockpile of God-wonders and God-thoughts*" (Psalm 40:5). As I walk through the wonders of God's creation I will not hear the birds sing, feel the refreshing breezes, see the wonderful sun sets, or touch or smell all that He has created for me today unless I live with hope and witness the miracles of creation. The hurts of the past and the fears of the future will block out God's blessings of the present unless I live now with hope.

I have found that in the midst of overwhelming odds I must not lose hope. **I must let God's power at work this day**

flow into my very being. I need to know in the depths of my soul that even though the dark nights of injustice surround me, the bright dawn of deliverance will soon arrive.

Archbishop Oscar Romeo declared prior to his death by an assassin's bullet, "Don't be led astray either by the allure of power and money or by following false ideologies. True hope is not found there either. True hope is not found in a revolution of violence and bloodshed, and hope is not found in money and power—neither on the left nor on the right. The hope that we must account for and that makes us speak with valor is found in Christ, who reigns even after death, even after murderous death. And with Him reign all who have preached his justice, his love, his hope, and his peace."

When I am feeling overwhelmed with the hurt, pain, injustices and hopelessness of life, I know from experience that when I call out unto the Lord, **He will answer.** It is like a literal fulfillment of Isaiah 43:20-21 where God says, "*I provide water in the desert and streams in the wasteland, to* *give drink to my people, my chosen, the people I formed for myself that they may proclaim my praise."*

The person who has learned to live with hope is the person who is living in the conscious presence of God's miraculous power. In the awareness of God's eternal presence and power, we are awakened to His love. This love is demonstrated not only through the wonders of creation, but also through the reality proclaimed in the Scriptures. There we learn that God has sent His son, the resurrected Christ, who plows daily through our hopeless circumstances, planting seeds of life both now and for all eternity.

Yes, the deserts and wastelands can be found among the homeless on the streets. It can also be found in the loneliness of the jail cell, the nursing home and the hospital bed. This brokenness is all around us. Dr. Martin Luther King, Jr. stated, "We have lived under the agony and darkness of Good Friday with the conviction that one day the heightened glow of Easter would emerge on the horizon."

This glow of glory has come. We are free to live in hope and experience the miracle of Christ's resurrection. Now He tells us, *"I tell you the truth, whoever hears my word and believes Him who sent me has eternal life and will not be condemned; he has crossed over from death to life. I tell you the truth, a time is coming and has now come when the dead will hear the voice of the Son of God and those who hear will live"* (John 5:24-25).

This is your day to begin to live. You can live in the hope that brings forth miracles if you only believe it when Jesus said in Mark 11:22-24, *"'Have faith in God, I tell you the truth, if anyone says to this mountain, 'Go, throw yourself into the sea,' and does not doubt in their heart but believes that what they say will happen, it will be done for them. Therefore I tell you, whatever you ask for in prayer, believe that you have received it, and it will be yours.'"*

If you believe these words of Jesus and act upon them then **today is your day for miracles**. The first thing Jesus said in

Mark 11:22 is *"Have faith in God."* He is not simply giving advice. He doesn't say it would be nice if we had faith, or He prefers we have faith. He is commanding us to *"have faith in God."*

I have personally witnessed countless miracles during the past 52 years as God has miraculously provided healing, financial help in times of need, and lives transformed through the resurrection power of Jesus Christ. What a mighty God we serve.

The one thing we can do the most to honor God is to have faith in Him. Hebrews 11:6 says, *"Without faith it is impossible to please God, because anyone who comes to Him must believe that He exists and that He rewards those who earnestly seek Him."*

Over and over the Bible tells us that faith is the way to experience miracles. Won't you take God at His word and let hope be born within you as you speak to that mountain of need and command it by faith in Jesus Christ to be thrown into the sea? The Bible shows us that with God all things are possible.

To the Canaanite woman who interceded for her demon possessed daughter Jesus said, *"Woman you have great faith! Your request is granted.' And her daughter was healed from that very hour"* (Matthew 15:28). Like this woman may our faith and love compel us to believe God for miracles in the lives of the hurting, hungry and homeless.

If more people prayed and then stepped forward by faith we would see the miraculous unfold to the extent no one would be homeless in America tonight. If churches would move forth and open the doors to the homeless lives would be saved and revival could come forth. Helping the hurting and homeless takes faith and without faith we can't please God. *"Everything that does not come from faith is sin"* (Romans 14:23).

Faith grows by knowing and acting on the word of God, because *"...faith comes by hearing, and hearing by the Word* *of God"* (Romans 10:17). If you are facing an impossible situation I encourage you to look at what God did for David when he confronted the giant Goliath by faith. Take another look at what God did for the city of Jerusalem in Hezekiah's day when Sennacherib's army surrounded the city and threatened to destroy it. The city stood steadfast with faith in God, who in turn miraculously saved the city.

Remember the story of Daniel and how God delivered him when he was thrown in the lion's den? Why are you so scared of being locked up or ridiculed when it comes to civil disobedience in the fight for justice in behalf of the homeless and down trodden? After all didn't Jesus say in Mark 11:24, *"Therefore I tell you, whatever you ask for in prayer, believe that you have received it, and it will be yours."*

As men and women of hope we pray in the name of Jesus. Peter Kreeft points out that, "The prayer of Jesus name actually brings God closer, makes Him more present. He is always present in some way, since He knows and loves each of us at every moment; but he is not present to those who do not pray as intimately as He is present to those who do. Prayer makes a difference; 'prayer changes things.' It may or may not change our external circumstances. (It does if God sees that change is good for us; it does not if God sees that it is not.) But it always changes our relationship to God, which is infinitely more important than external circumstances, however pressing they may seem, because it's eternal but they are temporary, and because it is our very self but they are not."

The development of our relationship with God may be that miracle He has for us today. After all what miracle could be greater than intimately knowing the Creator and Redeemer of heaven and earth? As we experience the miracle of a deeper relationship with God through Jesus Christ we will awaken to the eternal presence of God and the changes He wants to bring about in our lives.

Mother Teresa gives us this insight into the miracle of prayer when she said, "love to pray – feel the need to pray often during the day and take the trouble to pray. If you want to pray better, you must pray more. Prayer enlargens the heart until it is capable of containing God's gift of himself. We need to find God and He cannot be found in noise and restlessness. See how nature, the trees, the flowers, the grass grow in perfect silence. See the stars, the moon and the sun, how they move in silence. Is not our mission to give God to the poor? Not a dead God but a Living, Loving God. The more we receive in silent prayer, the more we can give in our active life."

Prayer birthed in the compassion of Jesus moves us among those in need. This enables us to experience that need in the depths of our souls. As we see so many hurting and homeless people it causes us to obey our Lord's command when He says "Ask the Lord of the harvest to send workers into His harvest field." Please pray for additional NLEC workers to come forth at this time.

As we see the magnitude of need around us, let us cry out with the prophet, *"My eyes fail from weeping, I am in torment within, my heart is poured out on the ground because my people are destroyed, because children and infants faint in the streets of the city"* (Lamentations 2:11). The miracle of compassion causes me to ask what would happen if I became desperate enough to wrestle with God like Jacob, if necessary, until my heart was broken over the pain of this generation of children and youth whom Satan has ravaged? As I hear story after story about the terrible things people are doing to each other, I find myself asking what would happen if I were prepared to engage in the spiritual warfare necessary to see people set free from satanic chains that hold them in bondage?

I must accept the fact that I can't really pray effectively without the Holy Spirit's help for, *"The Spirit helps us in our weakness. We do not know what we ought to pray for"* (Romans 8:26).

Josef Pieper in his book entitled, "On Hope," states, "Christ is the actual foundation of hope. In a striking sentence the letter to the Hebrews speaks of the hope we have "...*as a sure and firm anchor of the soul, reaching even behind the veil, where our forerunner Jesus has entered for us*" (Hebrews 6:19). Thomas Aquinas comments: "Christ has entered for us into the inner sanctuary of the tent and there made firm our hope."

Because Christ is risen, we have the gift of hope. This reality is demonstrated through every seed that is planted and then resurrected into a wonderful plant with the purpose planned at the time of its creation. The Creator of all commands through His creation and the power of His word, "*Do not fear; for I am with you; do not be dismayed, for I am your God. I will strengthen you and Help you; I will uphold you with my righteous right hand*" (Isaiah 41:10).

The fact that God upholds us with His righteous right hand tells us we do not need to be afraid of life. Present circumstances cannot suffocate our hope for the future, because Jesus has risen from death and we now have hope for all eternity.

Perhaps something or someone in your past plucked away at your self-esteem, feather by feather, until you stood naked and defenseless in the world. All that is left is rage, fear, and anger living in an unforgiving heart. As a result, sadness is kept locked behind the door of your life.

The time has come to stop denying the hurt and then, once acknowledging it, stop blaming others for it. Start all over and **let the love and hope of Jesus Christ heal you now.**

As long as you continue to hold on to your bitterness, you will continue to be a victim. Yes, you were deeply hurt in the past, but that fact is you cannot change the past. What you can change is your perception of it and the feelings which enslave you in the present. That is why you need to receive God's gift of hope and respond in a positive way to the invitation that Jesus gives in Matthew 11:28 when He says, "*Come to Me, all of you who are weary and burdened and I will give you rest.*"

When I get all wrapped up in the memories of the past or the worries of the future I am not able to experience God's hope in the present. Worry keeps me from experiencing the wonders of God's creation in the present. It fills me so full of self—there is no room for God. When there is no room for God there is no room for other people. This worry and fear can drive me to depression or a self-centered spirituality that does not include the needs of others. That is why I must spend time alone with the Lord in prayer and daily Bible reading.

The fact is that even though we know that the death of Jesus Christ has provided the solution for sin and His resurrected body opened the door to an eternal hope for us, we still live in a very troubled world. That troubled world also invades regularly our inner world, robbing us of the reality that we can live in hope. Paul reawakens us to the future that hope provides in the midst of our present circumstances when He declared, *"We rejoice in the hope of the glory of God. Not only so, but we also rejoice in our sufferings, because we know that suffering produces perseverance; perseverance, char-acter; and character, hope. And hope does not disappoint us, because God has poured out His love into our hearts by the Holy Spirit, whom He has given us"* (Romans 5:2-5).

If we have received Jesus Christ as Lord and Savior of our life, then we need to learn to live with the hope He has provided for us. **This hope frees us to love and be loved.** For without the free flow of such love we will find ourselves growing old in a lifeless world without hope both now and for all eternity.

Dig into the Word of God and learn how living in hope is a result of faith and prayer.

1. What instructions does Isaiah 43:18-19 give us concerning the pain we have experienced in the past?

2. In order to live with hope, what does 2 Corinthians 10:5 say I must do?

3. According to Archbishop Oscar Romeo where is true hope found?

4. In John 5:24-25 how does one receive eternal life?

5. What happens when we have faith in God according to Mark 11:22-24?

6. How did Jesus respond in Matthew 15:28 to the Canaanite woman?

7. According to Romans 10:17 how does faith come?

8. What does Mother Teresa say we must do if we want to pray better?

9. What does prayer in the compassion of Jesus do to us?

10. How does the Holy Spirit help us pray effectively according to Romans 8:26?

Planting the Seeds of Hope and Love
Chapter 11

So many are depressed at this moment because the pain of the past and unmet expectations of the present have removed all real hope for the future. As a result, all they can think about is how they are going to escape the present hopeless situation they are in. The problem of just leaving the present circumstances is it provides no real solution. The key is learning how to plant seeds of hope.

If I am going to do that, I cannot afford to listen to those crazy tapes of bitterness and hopelessness going around in my brain. I must believe and receive it when Jesus says, *"I've come to set the captives free."* It is that freedom which will allow the seeds of hope and love to be planted in me.

Proverbs 23:7 says, *"As a man (that includes a woman also) thinketh in his (or her) heart so he (or she) is."* From this verse we see that our feelings, passions and behavior are controlled by the way we think and speak. If we let our minds be filled with the stinking thinking of the toxic poison of hatred and hopelessness we will never be able to have the seeds of hope planted in us. That is why we are told in 2 Corinthians 10:5 to *"Cast down imaginations, and every high thing that exalts itself against the knowledge of God, and bringing in to captivity every thought to the obedience of Christ."*

An example of someone who planted these seeds of hope in the midst of what could have been a life of despair and hopelessness was Leah. She was Jacob's first wife. Leah was unattractive, unwanted, and unloved by her husband. Jacob had worked for Leah's father Laban in order to marry his younger daughter Rachel. On the wedding night, Laban put Leah, his older daughter in the marriage tent and Jacob had to work another seven years for Rachel. The scriptures tell us that Rachel was loved by Jacob but Leah was hated. Genesis 29:31 tell us that *"The Lord saw that Leah was unloved (hated)…"*

The exciting thing about studying the Bible is that we see over and over that God is drawn to those who hurt. He saw Leah's pain, loneliness and heartache. Leah realized this when she gave birth to her first son. In verse 32 of Genesis 29 we see her saying, *"Now...my husband will love me."* But Jacob still didn't love her. Twice more she gave birth to sons but Jacob still didn't care for her.

Leah was learning she couldn't make her husband love her. The harder she would try, as she continued to be jealous of Jacob's love toward her sister Rachel, the worse things got. Finally a miracle of grace occurred within her. She allowed the seeds of hope to be planted in the love God had for her. As she drew closer to the Lord Leah became pregnant a fourth time. In Genesis 29:35 she says *"Now I will praise the Lord."* She named the child Judah which means "praise." It was from the line of Judah that Jesus was born.

Leah learned that as she moved from hopelessness, jealousy, and self-fulfillment, she could be a worshipper of God. As she worshipped Him and planted seeds of hope in the ground of His love she entered life's highest fulfillment. As a result a true inner beauty began to grow in Leah and she became irresistible to Jacob. In fact, we find in Genesis 49:29-31, that Jacob charges his sons to take his body after he dies back to Canaan and put it in the cave of Ephron next to Leah.

Now, you and I have the God in whose love Leah planted her seeds of hope telling us, *"Do not fear; for I am with you; do not be dismayed, for I am your God. I will strengthen you and help you; I will uphold you with my righteous right hand"* (Isaiah 41:10).

The fact that God upholds us with His righteous right hand tells us we do not need to be afraid of life. **Present circumstances cannot suffocate our hope for a future,** for the resurrected Christ has planted the seeds of hope for a future both now and for all eternity in our hearts.

We live in a very troubled world that invades our inner world, robbing us of the reality that we have a future filled with hope. Paul reawakens us to the future that hope provides in the midst of our present circumstances when he declared, *"We rejoice in the hope of the glory of God. Not only so, but we also rejoice in our sufferings, because we know that suffering produces perseverance; perseverance, character; and character, hope. And hope does not disappoint us, because God has poured out His love into our hearts by the Holy Spirit, whom He has given us"* (Romans 5:2-5).

If you have received Jesus Christ as Lord and Savior of your life, then you have the seed of hope planted in you. This hope frees you to love and be loved. Without the free flow of such love you will find yourself growing old in a lifeless world without hope for a future.

Hopelessness wears us down as we travel through life. Yet when we have hope burning within, we have a refuge which keeps the heart of love from hardening. *"We do not lose heart. Though outwardly we are wasting away, yet inwardly we are being renewed day by day"* (2 Corinthians 4:16). The Message Bible expresses this verse in the following fashion: *"We're not giving up. How could we! Even though on the outside it often looks like things are falling apart on us, on the inside, where God is making new life, not a day goes by without His unfolding grace."*

With the seeds of hope growing within us, the bills may be mounting, but the reality that, *"My God will meet all my needs according to His glorious riches in Christ Jesus"* (Philippians 4:19), provides a present peace and a hope for the future that passes all understanding. This happens as we *"...fix our eyes on Jesus, the author and perfecter of our faith, who for the joy set before Him endured the cross, scorning its shame and sat down at the right hand of the throne of God. Consider Him who endured such opposition from sinful men, so that you will not grow weary and lose heart"* (Hebrews 12:2-3).

The lies that feed our stinking thinking have just enough truth to make them appear as truth. In reality such lies are a toxic poison that prevent us from doing the good that is so urgently needed.

A steady diet of the toxins of negative thinking and speaking is deadly. In Romans 8:6, Paul clearly points out that the mind set on the flesh is death when he says, *"The mind of sinful man is death, but the mind controlled by the Spirit is life and peace."*

If we want to have the seeds of hope planted in us so we can share hope in word and deed, we must stop listening to the crazy tapes of negativism and hopelessness. Instead we should do what Philippians 4:8 tells us to do when it declares, *"Whatsoever things that are true, whatsoever things are honest, whatsoever things are just, whatsoever things are pure, whatsoever things are lovely, whatsoever things are a good report; if there be any virtue, and if there be any praise think on these things."* By doing this we will allow our pain to be transformed through Christ's resurrection rather than letting it be transferred to others by our stinking thinking and lousy speaking.

Filtering our thoughts through God's eternal love demonstrated through Jesus Christ, goes a long way towards giving us the power to plant seeds of hope in others. The end result of such filtering, results in thoughts and words of thanksgiving. 2 Corinthians 9:15, *"Thanks be to God for His indescribable gift."*

Believers in the one true God are encouraged to *"...give thanks in all circumstances"* (1 Thessalonians 5:18), *"...give thanks to God the Father for everything"* (Ephesians 5:19-20), and present prayers and petitions *"...with thanksgiving to God"* (Philippians 4:6-7).

God has given all of us the opportunity to plant seeds of hope and love with thanksgiving. At New Life Evangelistic Center, we plant these seeds of hope as we share the gospel by giving out food, water, hygiene kits and then helping those without anywhere to go, to have a place to stay in one of the NLEC safe houses. It is such a blessing to see the NLEC teams of men and woman planting their seeds of hope in a wide variety of ways on a daily basis. This multi-racial team is united through the love of Christ and the power of the Holy Spirit.

Whatever seeds of hope and love you plant now will continue to live on both now and for all eternity. Henry Ward Beecher expressed this fact by pointing out that "when the sun finally drops below the horizon in the early evening, evidence of its work remains. The skies continue to glow for a full hour after its departure."

"In the same way when a good or a great person's life comes to its final sunset, the skies of this world are illuminated until long after he is out of view. Such a person does not die from this world for when he departs he leaves much of himself behind, and being dead, he still speaks."

God has given each and every one of us the opportunity to plant the seeds of hope and love in the midst of this landscape of helplessness and despair. As we do this we will begin to realize that Christ has chosen us in the midst of this time of political hostility to manifest His love. When this miracle takes place, we will see Him do exceedingly far more than what we can ask or think.

The Holy Spirit loves to take ordinary people such as you and me to do extra ordinary things as He did with Moses, Peter, and Stephen. In their lives, we see individuals who were set free from hopelessness to the extent they were able to do great things for the glory of God. This is a result of committing one's life to Christ as Peter declared in Acts 4:12, "*Salvation is found in no one else, for there is no other name under heaven given to men by which we must be saved.*" Such a commitment sets us free from the paralysis of fear in order that we may, in this time and place, be God's instruments of hope and healing.

God often trains his great men and women by placing them first in insignificant positions, in order that they may ultimately do the great work that He has called them to do. For Stephen this meant being involved in the distribution of food to the needy. Moses was tending the flock of his father-in-law when God spoke to him through a burning bush. Then He has

Moses return to Egypt to liberate the children of Israel.

God's response to this world that is intoxicated by its lust for power, is powerlessness. God chose to enter into human history as hope and love wrapped in a little baby. In this tiny powerless baby, who is completely dependent on his parents, we discover the power of God to plant seeds of hope and love.

That is the mystery of the incarnation. God became human, to break through the walls of power in total weakness and in the most hopeless situations plant His seeds. How does the story end? On a cross, where the same human person hangs naked with nails through his hands and feet.

The powerlessness of the **manger** has become the powerlessness of the cross. People jeer at him, laugh at him, spit in his face and shout: *"He saves others, he cannot save himself! If he is the King of Israel, let him come down from the cross* *now, and we will believe in him"* (Matthew 27: 42).

Jesus is the celebration of hope, which He provided through His resurrection from the dead. His coming was prophesied to bring a social revolution where his Kingdom would turn things upside down: *"The mighty would be brought low, the rich sent away empty, the poor exalted, the hungry satisfied"* (Luke 1: 52-53).

Jesus identified himself with the weak, the outcast, the downtrodden; the ones who have lost their ability to dream. His Kingdom undermines all economic systems that reward the rich and punish the poor. It is Jesus, who gives hope and love to the helpless, hurting and homeless. In Luke 6: 24-25 Jesus declared, *"Woe to you that are rich for you have received your consolation. Woe to you that are full now for you shall hunger."* Jesus sets free those whose only hope consisted of getting more money and things. Luke 12:15 says, *"Take heed and beware of all covetousness; for a man's life does not consist in the abundance of his possessions."*

Because of the life, death, and resurrection of Jesus Christ, no matter how poor, homeless or sick you may be, **you can dare to have hope in spite of your failures.** This is possible because Christ is Risen.

As we get older and our bodies get weaker it becomes increasingly critical that we are anchored in the hope that God is able to make our impossible dreams a reality. Moses had to learn this as he was called forth at the age of eighty to deliver the children of Israel from captivity. Abraham had to accept the fact that God was able to make him the father of a great nation when he was over ninety years of age. Romans 4:21 says that Abraham was "...*being fully persuaded that God had power to do what He had promised.*"

If you are going to accomplish that which God has called us to do you must have hope and be fully persuaded that God is able to make your impossible dreams come true. Then we must accept the power that Paul speaks of in Ephesians 3:20 when he says, "*Now to Him who is able to do immeasurably more than all we ask or imagine, according to His power that is at work within us.*"

In order to understand this power at work we must have the seeds of hope planted in us and know what it means to be in Christ Jesus. 2 Corinthians 5:17 says, "*If anyone is in Christ, he is a new creation; the old has gone, the new has come!*"

This hope is a result of repenting of our sins and committing our lives to Jesus and living daily under His direction. As a result, we are not just reformed, rehabilitated or re-educated, but we are **recreated** (a new creation) living in union with Jesus Christ. "*So then, just as we received Christ Jesus as Lord, continue to live in Him, rooted and built up in Him, strengthened in the faith as you were taught, and overflowing with thankfulness*" (Colossians 2:6-7).

If you have the seeds of hope planted in you as a result of being fully persuaded that God loves you then there is no limit to what God can do through you. Sure, you may encounter difficulties but *"Do not lose heart. Though outwardly we are wasting away, yet inwardly we are being renewed day by day. For our light and momentary troubles are achieving for us an eternal glory that far outweighs them all. So, we fix our eyes not on what is seen, but on what is unseen. For what is seen, is temporary, but what is unseen is eternal"* (2 Corinthians 4:16-18).

As children of the living God we let the word of God plant the seeds of hope deep within our hearts in order that we may share this hope with others. This will happen as we move forth and *"Remember we live by faith, not by sight"* (2 Corinthians 5:6). *"In the power of God: with weapons of righteousness in the right hand and in the left;"* (2 Corinthians 6:7).

With the power of the resurrected Christ deep within us we can, with faith and courage, pursue the dream He has given us to be His instruments of **faith**, **hope** and **love**.

Plant seeds of hope within you by answering the following.

1. How are our feelings, passions and behavior controlled by the way we think or speak according to Proverbs 23:7?

2. If we are going to have hope planted in us what does 2 Corinthians 10:5 say we must do?

3. How is Leah an example of someone who planted seeds of hope in the midst of despair and hopelessness?

4. What assurance does Isaiah 41:10 give?

5. According to Romans 5:2-5 how can we rejoice in our suffering?

6. What is happening on the inside of us according to 2 Corinthians 4:16 as presented in the Message Bible?

7. How does Philippians 4:19 give me hope when I have bills I don't know how I am going to pay?

8. According to Philippians 4:8 what things should we be thinking about?

9. What is God able to do according to Ephesians 3:20?

10. How do we continue to have hope and not lose heart considering 2 Corinthians 4:16-18?

How to Have Hope When You Are at the End of Your Rope
Chapter 12

How many times have you cried out for help when you felt all the pressures have pushed you over the cliff of life? There you are hanging at the end of your hope. You knew you had to hang on because you were at the end of your rope. If you turned loose you were going to drop into a bottomless pit of hopelessness.

When you feel you are at the end of your hope it all comes down to the same word spelled STRESS. Jesus declared in John 16:33, *"In this world you will have trouble. But take heart! I have overcome the world."*

Right now in those areas of our life where it seems everything is crumbling into the valley of hopelessness Jesus wants us to reach out to Him in prayer. Believe that He has overcome the world. Remember, *"Hope does not disappoint us, because God has poured out His love into our hearts by the Holy Spirit, whom He has given us...God demonstrates His own love for us in this: While we were still sinners, Christ died for us"* (Romans 5:5 & 8).

When you are at the end of your rope and feel you can no longer have hope, don't give up, give it to God. It's a fact that everyday God does so many things for us, and we don't even recognize it as a manifestation of His love. Take for example the rising of the sun. If it did not rise after a few days all life as we know it would start to die on planet earth. God has the sun rise each day for you. Now in the midst of the toxic stress that may seem to be choking all life out of you, declare to believe in Romans 5:8, that *"...while we were still sinners, Christ died for us."*

With the realization that Christ died for you, accept the fact that you *"...are God's handiwork, created in Christ Jesus to do good works, which God prepared in advance for us to do"* (Ephesians 2:10).

You won't be able to accomplish these good works if you continue to live under the cloud of toxic stress that makes you feel you are constantly at the end of your rope. I would like to take four tools from God's tool repair kit, and let the Holy Spirit, through the power of the Risen Christ, give you the ability to begin living a victorious life filled with hope.

1. **God's purpose for your life:**

    Begin to picture God's **purpose** for your life. As you pursue this purpose let it be done with the peace of Christ that passes all understanding. *"'For I was hungry and you gave me something to eat, I was thirsty and you gave me something to drink, I was a stranger and you invited me in, I needed clothes and you clothed me, I was sick and you looked after me, I was in prison and you came to visit me.' Then the righteous will answer him, 'Lord, when did we see you hungry and feed you, or thirsty and give you something to drink? When did we see you a stranger and invite you in, or needing clothes and clothe you? When did we see you sick or in prison* *and go to visit you?' The King will reply, 'Truly I tell you, whatever you did for one of the least of these brothers and sisters of mine, you did for me'"* (Matthew 25:35-40).

2. **Pray:**
Don't panic, instead **pray** specifically for the needs that you are facing. Directions for such stress-free praying are clearly given in Philippians 4:6-7 where it tells us to *"...not be anxious about anything, but in every situation, by prayer and petition, with thanksgiving, present your requests to God. And the peace of God, which transcends all understanding, will guard your hearts and minds in Christ Jesus."*

3. **Pace Yourself:**
Prioritize your time and **pace** yourself. Learn to guard your time wisely. Satan will constantly speak condemnation, so you must remember that there is no condemnation for those who are in Christ Jesus. Spend time in prayer

and Bible reading each day. Exercise, eat nourishing meals and get plenty of sleep. Protect your time to rest in the Lord and then move forth with the strength and anointing He provides. As you pace yourself according to His word watch Him do exceedingly beyond what you can ask or think. Proverbs 4:26 says, *"Give careful thought to the paths for your feet and be steadfast in all your ways."*

4. **Experience Christ's Peace:**

Experience Christ's **peace** as you come to Him in the midst of life's struggles. Accept His invitation to come into the divine rest that only He can give at those moments when hopelessness overshadows you. *"Come to me, all of you who are weary and burdened, and I will give you rest. Take my yoke upon you and learn from me, for I am gentle and humble in heart, and you will find rest for your souls. For my yoke is easy and my burden is light"* (Matthew 11:28-30).

Oh the peace that awaits us from all the hopelessness that is wearing us down and out. This peace takes place once we are convinced as Paul was of God's love and the hope it provides. He declared, *"In all these things we are more than conquerors through Him who loved us. For I am convinced that neither death nor life, neither angels nor demons, neither the present nor the future, nor any powers, neither height nor depth, nor anything else in all creation, will be able to separate us from the love of God that is in Christ Jesus our Lord"* (Romans 8:37-39).

The love God has for you is the very foundation of hope. The question is will you receive this love He has for you? Satan is constantly trying to offer cheap substitutes for this eternal love that God provides. When one becomes sick and tired of such substitutes and desires God's love, then the enemy tries to make them feel they are not worthy of such. In order to combat Satan's lies and feeling of hopelessness we must know the Word of God.

When I am at the end of my rope without hope **I must earnestly pray and remember** that, *"...there is now no condemnation for those who are in Christ Jesus"* (Romans 8:1).

When Satan tries to stress you out and get you to believe that if you are just good enough or work hard enough you will have hope, you need to rise up and declare, "devil you are a liar. I am sick and tired of the condemnation you have placed on me. I am tired of the rat race of hopelessness you have placed me in. I am accepting, according to the word of God, God's love for me and the hope it provides. I am a child of God liberated through the blood of Jesus Christ from condemnation, stress and hopelessness. As Romans 8:37 says, *"I am more than a conqueror through Christ who loves me."*

There have been many times when I have felt like anything but a conqueror. That is why I must follow the directives given in Hebrews 10:35-36 when it says, *"...do not throw away your confidence, it will be richly rewarded. You need to persevere so that when you have done the will of God, you will receive what He has promised."*

Henri Nouwen in his book, "With Open Hands" explains how prayer frees us to experience in a new way the reality of this love of God. Nouwen stated, "Praying is no easy matter. It demands a relationship in which you allow someone other than yourself to enter into the very center of your being, to be there when you would rather live in darkness, and to touch there what you would rather leave untouched."

"The resistance to praying is like the resistance of tightly clenched fists. The image shows a tension, a desire to cling tightly to yourself, a greediness which betrays fear. When you want to pray, then the first question is: How do I open my closed hands? Perhaps you can find your ways to prayer by carefully listening to the words of the angel to Zechariah, Mary, the frightened shepherds, and the woman at the tomb: 'Don't be afraid of the One who wants to enter your most intimate space and invite you to let go of what you are clinging to so anxiously.'"

"Each time you dare to let go and surrender one of those many fears, your hand opens a little and your palms spread out in a gesture of receiving. It is a long spiritual journey of trust, for behind each fist, another is hiding and sometimes the process seems endless. Much has happened in your life to make all those fists, and any hour of the day or night you might find yourself clenching your fists again out of fear. Maybe someone will say to you, 'You have to forgive yourself.' But that isn't possible. What is possible is to open your hands without fear, so the One who loves you can blow your sins away."

With Nouwen's words in mind I would like to return to 1 John 4:16 & 18, which declares, *"And so we know and rely on the love God has for us. God is love. Whoever lives in love lives in God, and God in Him. There is no fear in love. But perfect love drives out fear."*

If I am going to cope with the toxic hopelessness in my life, I must be consistently conscious of God's love. This love is revealed not only in His wonderful works of creation but in the fact declared in John 3:16 that *"God so loved the world that He gave His one and only Son, that whoever believes in Him shall not perish but have eternal life."*

It is the realization of God's love for me which triggers within me love and hope for others as explained in 1 John 4:19-21. *"We love because He first loved us. If anyone says, 'I love God,' yet hates his brother, he is a liar. For anyone who does not love his brother, whom he has seen, cannot love God, whom he has not seen. And He has given us this command: Whoever loves God must also love his brother."*

As I let the love of God flow in me and through me into a hurting world I will be a living instrument proclaiming the love of Christ in word and deed. As I do this I will discover a **purpose for living** that gives me **hope to persevere under stress.**

1 John 4:7-10 tells us, *"Dear friends, let us love one another, for love comes from God. Everyone who loves has been born of*

God and knows God. Whoever does not love does not know God, because God is love. This is how God showed his love among us; He sent His one and only Son into the world that we might live through Him. This is love; not that we loved God, but that He loved us and sent His Son as an atoning sacrifice for our sins."

This knowledge that God loves you enables you to boldly face life by praying with power and living a life of hope. **When you know God loves you**, you don't have to get stressed out about failure because He has promised to never leave you nor forsake you.

Now as you grasp hold of the fact God loves you, your healing of hopelessness can begin. The main reason God can't give us His hope is because we are so busy trying to get it ourselves. If we do arrive at some kind of hope on our own it isn't long and this hope vanishes or only drives us further from Him. God loves us too much for that. When we realize that every good thing comes from God we are free to receive His love and His hope that passes all understanding.

It is the love of God, which heals us of our hopelessness. His love also gives us the ability to love others. With God's love dwelling in us we will receive the strength to have hope in spite of the circumstances.

There are people only you can minister His love to. Now ask Christ to show you how to do it. Spend time with the Lord daily praying, reading the Bible, and observing creation. Let His love flow in you and through you. Just let God fill you with hope as you enter into His rest and experience the peace and reassurance that He has everything under control.

Remember "...*a heart of peace gives life to the body...*" (Proverbs 14:30). "*Those who hope in the Lord will renew their strength. They will soar on wings like eagles; they will run and not grow weary, they will walk and not faint*" (Isaiah 40:31).

The time has come for us to just relax and fall into the hands of our loving Heavenly Father. **God is love and has a**

plan for our lives. We need to turn loose and let the peace of our Lord Jesus Christ sweep over us. After all, He has promised and has demonstrated through His death and resurrection that He will never leave us nor forsake us.

In Philippians 4:6-9 Paul tells us how to have hope when we are at the end of our rope, "*Do not be anxious about anything, but in every situation, by prayer and petition, with thanksgiving, present your requests to God. And the peace of God, which transcends all understanding, will guard your hearts and your minds in Christ Jesus. Finally, brothers and sisters, whatever is true, whatever is noble, whatever is right, whatever is pure, whatever is lovely, whatever is admirable – if anything is excellent or praiseworthy – think about such things. Whatever you have learned or received or heard from me, or seen in me – put it into practice. And the God of peace will be with you.*"

You no longer have to spend the rest of your life feeling like you are hanging without hope at the end of your rope. Turn loose and fall into the everlasting arms of the God of hope.

Now "..*may the God of hope fill you with all joy and peace as you trust in Him, so that you may overflow with hope by the power of the Holy Spirit*" (Romans 15:13).

To stop hanging without hope at the end or your rope please answer the following.

1. According to Romans 5:5 & 8 how can we have hope when we feel we are at the end of our rope?

2. What do you feel is your purpose for life?

3. Directions for stress-free praying are given in Philippians 4:6-7. What are they?

4. Why is pacing yourself and living in Christ's peace so important when it comes to having hope when you feel you are at the end of your rope?

5. The love God has for you is the very foundation of hope. How is this explained in Romans 8:37-39?

6. According to Henri Nouwen how does prayer free us to experience in a new way the reality of God's love for us?

7. How does God's love trigger within us love and hope for others according to 1 John 4:19-21?

8. In light of John 4:7-10 in what way did God show His love among us?

9. Why should that motivate us to love others?

10. What directions does Paul give us in Philippians 4:6-9 on how to have hope when we are at the end of our rope?

When it Comes to Hope Where is Your Head At?
Chapter 13

The statement, "Where is your head at?" is actually a reference to where is your mind at or what are you thinking about? Since the mind is the control tower for your life, what you think not only directs who you are and what you do but determines what you think about God, others, yourself and life in general.

We can't control other people or the circumstances we face in life, but we can choose to let our thoughts be filtered by the Holy Spirit through the word of God. As we do this He will give us the hope and wisdom on how to perceive these situations and respond in a Christ like way.

Colossians 3:2 tells us to set our mind "...*on the things above, not on the things that are on the earth.*" The only way to do this is to immerse ourselves in the word of God.

Proverbs 23:7 says, "*As a man (that includes a woman also) thinketh in his (or her) heart so he (or she) is."* **The Bible clearly teaches that a person's feelings, passions and behavior is controlled by the way he or she thinks and speaks.** If a person's mind is filled with the toxic poison of negativism then all they do and say will reflect such. That is why we are told in 2 Corinthians 10:5 to *"...cast down imaginations, and every high thing that exalteth itself against the knowledge of God, and bringing into captivity every thought to the obedience of Christ."*

Bringing every thought to the obedience of hope in Christ will totally transform your life. That is why we are told in Romans 12:2, *"Do not conform to the pattern of this world, but be transformed by the renewing of your mind. Then you will be able to test and approve what God's will is—His good, pleasing and perfect will."* This verse is telling us that we need to renew our minds by filtering our thoughts through the hope coming from God's eternal love.

We have got to stop letting the disappointments of the past, the hopelessness of the present or the fears of the future determine the course of our lives. It is not these events but the way we think about them that determine who we are. What we tell ourselves concerning these events could be either a truth or a lie. That is why every thought, feeling and event must be filtered through God's hope, given through Jesus Christ, who is as John 14:6 says, "...*the way, the truth and the life.*"

William Backus and Marie Chapian state the following in their book, <u>Telling Yourself the Truth</u>. "Your beliefs and misbeliefs are the most important factors of your mental and emotional life. Disbelieving is the direct cause of emotional turmoil, maladaptive behavior and so-called mental illness. Misbelief is the cause of the destructive behavior people persist in engaging in even when they are fully aware that it is harmful to them (such as overeating, smoking, lying, drunkenness, stealing or adultery)."

The feelings of hopelessness that compose our thinking just have enough truth to make them appear as truth. In reality such feelings are a toxic poison that enslave us in destructive activities. It's a fact that if you tell yourself an untruth long enough it appears to be truth. James 3:15 tells us where this kind of thinking comes from. *"Such wisdom does not come down from heaven but is earthy, unspiritual, of the devil."* A steady diet of such toxins of hopeless thinking is deadly.

In Romans 8:6, Paul clearly points out that the mind set on the flesh is death. *"The mind of sinful man is death, but the mind controlled by the Spirit is life and peace."*

The words we say to ourselves can entrap us or empower us. Psychiatrist Willard Gaylin states, "A denigrated self-image is a tar baby. The more we play with it, embrace it, the more bound we are to do it." The time has come for us to listen to the words we tell ourselves and ask, "Am I building a tar baby?"

I have said and thought too often that things are hopeless when I should be thinking and saying, "I can have hope because I am trusting Jesus, who has saved me and has given me peace and hope."

If I am going to have hope as I face the future I must strive to keep my mind on Jesus and not listen to the crazy tapes of negativism and hopelessness. Instead I need to do what Philippians 4:8 tells me to do. There I see I need to filter my thoughts through God's eternal hope and think about, "...*whatsoever things that are true, whatsoever things are honest, whatsoever things are just whatsoever things are pure, whatsoever things are lovely, whatsoever things are a good report; if there be any virtue, and if there be any praise think on these things.*"

If I am not conscious where my head is at it is easy to give into the temptation to engage in either fight or flight. Such was the case for Mary and Martha when their brother Lazarus died. In John chapter 11 we see this event taking place.

It is moments like that when we must filter our thoughts through God's eternal hope and exercise the faith to:

1. **Get Jesus involved.**

2. **Know that Jesus cares.**

When hopeless thinking starts taking over we need to know that Jesus cares. In verse 35 of John 11 we read, "*Jesus wept.*"

3. **We must do our part.**

We must ask ourselves what is the main obstacle that is keeping me from putting my head in the right place and having hope things will improve? Then we must do our part. In this case Jesus told them to "...*take away the stone*" to Lazarus' grave.

4. **Watch Jesus do His part.**

Then exercise the faith and hope necessary and watch Jesus do His part. In verse 43 we see Jesus declaring, "*Lazarus come out.*"

5. **We must do our part again.**

We must remember that everything we go through has the purpose of strengthening our faith and hope for the future. As a result we must

<u>do our part again</u> and "...*take off the grave clothes and let him go*" (verse 44). We must take off the grave clothes of the sinful thought patterns of the past and clothe ourselves "...*with the Lord Jesus Christ and do not think about how to gratify the desires of the sinful nature*" (Romans 13:14).

By being clothed with Jesus Christ we are then freed to move from a life of hopeless thinking, into one where **faith is the victory.** This is the result of filtering our thoughts through the eternal hope God provides.

Getting our head in the right place and filtering our thoughts through Christ's eternal hope goes a long way towards cleaning our minds of the negative toxic poisons that can and will destroy us. The end result of such filtering results in **thoughts and words of thanksgiving and praise.**

Living the hope filled life involves giving thanks which cleanses our mind from the toxic poisons of a negative world. Dr.

Robert A. Emmons in his book <u>Thanks: How the Science of Gratitude Can Make You Happier</u> states, "Our groundbreaking research has shown that grateful people experience higher levels of positive emotions such as joy, enthusiasm, love, happiness, and optimism, and that the practice of gratitude as a discipline protects a person from the destructive impulses of envy, resentment, greed, and bitterness. Gratitude is a feeling that stems from certain perceptions and thoughts. Therefore, in order to become more grateful, we need to look at life in a certain way, and one tangible way we can do this is through the lens of gifts and giftedness."

It is easy to be thankful and filled with hope when we think about the gift of eternal life provided through Jesus Christ. *"Thanks be to God for His indescribable gift"* (2 Corinthians 9:15).

Believers in the eternal all encompassing love of God are then encouraged to *"...give thanks in all circumstances"* (1 Thessalonians 5:18), *"...give thanks to God the Father for everything"* (Ephesians 5:19-20), *"...present prayers and petitions 'with thanksgiving to God'"* (Philippians 4:6-7).

Emmons encourages people to get their heads in the right place by engaging in gratitude journalizing each night. This involves listing the things they are thankful for. His research shows that, "compared to those who were not jotting down their blessings nightly, participants in the gratitude condition reported getting more hours of sleep each night, spending less time awake before falling asleep, and feeling more refreshed upon awakening. Perhaps this is why grateful individuals feel more alive and vital during the day. This finding is enormous in that sleep disturbance and poor sleep quality has been identified as central indicators of poor overall well-being. People whose sleep is routinely disrupted have high levels of stress hormones and compromised immune function."

How we need to be a people who allow an **attitude of gratitude** with the thoughts of thanksgiving and praise be planted within us. That is why in Philippians 4:4-9 Paul said, *"Rejoice in the Lord always. I will say it again: Rejoice! Let your gentleness be evident to all. The Lord is near. Do not be anxious about anything, but in every situation, by prayer and petition, with thanksgiving, present your requests to God. And the peace of God, which transcends all understanding, will guard your hearts and your minds in Christ Jesus. Finally, brothers and sisters, whatever is true, whatever is noble, whatever is right, whatever is pure, whatever is lovely, whatever is admirable—if anything is excellent or praiseworthy—think about such things."*

As long as you hold on to your hopelessness and let anxiety control you, you will continue to be a victim. You may have been deeply hurt in the past, but the fact is you cannot change the past. What you can change is how you think about it and if you will respond in a hopeful way to the invitation that Jesus gives in Matthew 11:28 when He says, *"Come to Me, all of you who are weary and burdened and I will give you rest."* This is done as we continue to spend time alone with the Lord in prayer and daily Bible reading. This results in thinking about that which is **true**, **noble**, **right**, **pure**, **lovely**, **hopeful**, **admirable** and **praiseworthy** (see Philippians 4:8).

As we read the Scriptures we are introduced to people like Joseph (Genesis, Chapters 37-50) who received terrible mistreatment, yet he refused to let hopelessness consume him. After being thrown in a well by his brothers, sold into slavery by his master's wife, and ending up in prison, Joseph still refused to resume the role of a victim locked in the prison of hopelessness. When he became a leader in the land of Egypt with power to destroy the brothers who mistreated him, Joseph told them in Genesis 50:20, *"You intended to harm me, but God intended it for good to accomplish what is now being done, the saving of many lives. So then don't be afraid. I will provide for you and your children. And he reassured them and spoke kindly to them."*

Healing from the mistreatments in our past begins once we realize that we no longer have to justify ourselves. This is possible because we have already been justified by Jesus Christ on the cross. We can choose to get our head in the right place by meditating on this fact and filter all those bitter, negative thoughts through the love Jesus demonstrated by dying for our sins on the cross. Romans 3:24 says that you and I have been justified by His grace through the redemption that came by Christ Jesus.

Throughout the story of Joseph, we see the words, "...*the Lord was with Joseph.*" The fact is the Lord is also with you. The same Jesus who declared, "*Lo, I am with you always even to the end of the world,*" is with you right now in the middle of that hurt and bitterness over the mistreatment in the past.

At this very moment, make the promise of Romans 8:28 your very own. "*In all things God works for the good of those who love Him, who have been called according to His purpose.*"

The Bible says, "*A person reaps what he sows, whoever sows to please their *flesh, from the flesh will reap destruction; whoever sows to please the Spirit, from the Spirit will reap eternal life. Let us not become weary in doing good, for at the proper time we will reap a harvest if we do not give up. Therefore, as we have opportunity, let us do good to all people, especially to those who belong to the family of believers"* (Galatians 6:7-10).

We are told in these verses that the thoughts we sow will result in actions reaped. If we continue to sow thoughts of negativity and hopelessness that is what we will reap.

The time has come to get our heads in the right place. This will happen as we apply Romans 12:2 which we read earlier, *"Do not conform to the pattern of this world but be transformed by the renewing of your mind. Then you will be able to test and approve what God's will is – His good, pleasing and perfect will."*

When Jesus comes into our life we can't simply add Him to the way we used to think. We are going to have to get into the scriptures daily as we let the Holy Spirit transform us by the renewing of our minds. This transformation involves putting away the hopelessness that no longer fits our identity in Christ. As a new creation in Christ we will put our minds on the things that are above, which are filled with hope both now and for all eternity.

When you commit your life to Jesus and someone then asks you where your head is at, you will be able to say it is on Jesus and the hope He provides. No longer will you continue to conform to the hopeless pattern of this world. This is possible because the Holy Spirit is daily transforming you by the renewing of your mind and the knowledge there is hope because Christ is Risen.

Fill your mind with hope by answering the following.

1. How does Proverbs 23:7 indicate that a person's behavior and hope is controlled by the way he or she thinks?

2. According to Romans 12:2 why is the renewing of your mind so important?

3. Are you building a tar baby as explained by psychiatrist Willard Gaylin?

4. What does Philippians 4:8 say you must do if you want to maintain hope?

5. John 11 gives us a formula of 5 ways we can filter our thoughts through

God's eternal hope. What are these 5 ways?

6. How does an attitude of gratitude help us to live a hope filled life?

7. In what ways does gratitude journalizing each night help you sleep better?

8. What did Joseph do to prevent being locked up in a mental prison of hopelessness and bitterness?

9. According to Galatians 6:7-10 why should we not get weary in doing good?

10. When someone asks you where is your head at what should you be able to tell them?

Here's Hope
Chapter 14

There is a time when all of us need hope. Sometimes the need is greater than at other times.

You may have lost your job, your home, your loved ones. The greater the need the greater the urgency that we come to the one who can give us hope for a brighter future. He made the heavens, the earth and the mountains. He holds the stars in His hands and calls them by name. For that reason the Psalmist said in Psalm 121:1-2, *"I lift up my eyes to the mountains, where does my help come from? My help comes from the Lord, the Maker of heaven and earth."*

He is the one who parted the Red Sea, closed the mouths of lions, healed the sick, and raised the dead. When the enemies of the poor and homeless attack, as I try to do God's work of providing for them, I must never forget the many examples in scripture of how God ambushes enemy armies. When I feel my troubles twisting my stomach into knots, I have to let the peace which Jesus provided take control.

It is Jesus who walked on the water, turned water into wine, healed the lame and opened the eyes of the blind. He promised that **He would never leave us nor forsake us.** Jesus, who caused the demons to tremble and raised the dead to life, now promises that He is with us always even to the end of the world.

The Bible tells us, "*Do not be afraid or discouraged, for the Lord will personally go ahead of you. He will be with you; He will neither fail you nor abandon you*" (Deuteronomy 31:8).

People may leave you or me. They may abandon us when we need them most, but **Jesus never will.** In Romans 8:37-39 we are told, "*...in all these things we are more than conquerors through Him who loved us. For I am convinced that neither death nor life, neither angels nor demons, neither the present nor the future, nor any* *powers, neither height nor depth, nor anything else in all creation, will be able to separate us from the love of God that is in Christ Jesus our Lord."*

The Bible declares there is no reason for us to feel hopeless because God is with us. He is personally going before us and He has no plans to fail or abandon us. Nothing nor no one can separate us from the love of God which He has demonstrated through Jesus Christ.

Right now Jesus is saying, *"Here is the hope you need. Just trust me with all those worries and cares that are too heavy for you to carry. I want you to give them to me, every single one of them."* 1 Peter 5:7 says, *"Give all your worries and cares to God for He cares about you."*

Jesus is always right on time. He knows you need hope. So He declares, *"Just trust me. Haven't I told you that a small amount of faith, the size of a mustard seed, will move that mountain of need standing before you? Just release your faith ow and believe that I will meet your need"* (Matthew 17:20).

Romans 5:6-8 tells us that, *"When we were utterly helpless, Christ came at just the right time and died for us sinners. Now, most people would not be willing to die for an upright person, though someone might perhaps be willing to die for a person who is especially good. But God showed His love for us by sending Christ to die for us while we were still sinners."*

Now I want to encourage you to seek God with your whole heart. As you do that you will see Him miraculously intervene in such a powerful way that you will know that God is bigger than every problem.

He promises, *"If you look for me whole-heartedly you will find me"* (Jeremiah 29:18). God doesn't play hide-and-seek with us. He is right there saying, "Here's hope."

As you go on a prayer walk in the great outdoors look up into the sky. There you will see the clouds that Psalm 104 says God rides on and the light He wraps around Himself. Look around you and witness how He daily provides for the birds, flowers, rabbits and the rest of creation. Let the wonders of His creation give you hope that He will provide for you.

When you search the scriptures you will find the promises of God along with miracle after miracle where God performed the impossible. As you seek God and read the scriptures your **faith** and **hope** will **grow**.

Continue to seek God as you recall all the help God has provided for you in the past. Then be assured that He will continue to help you at this time of great need in your life.

Whatever you do don't give up praying. Over and over in the scriptures we are told to bring every need to God in prayer. In Matthew 7:7-8 Jesus says, *"Ask, and it will be given to you; seek and you will find; knock and the door will be opened to you. For everyone who asks receives, the one who seeks finds, and to him who knocks, the door will be opened."*

Perhaps at this moment you may feel like saying, "Lord, I'm exhausted. This is too much for me. I can't take it anymore. When I am this weary, Jesus, my mind starts playing tricks on me. I forget you are an everlasting God who doesn't grow tired or weary. You are the all-powerful One who gives strength to the weary and increases the power of the weak" (See Isaiah 40:28-29).

"I know with your help Almighty God that I can do all things through Christ Jesus, who strengthens me. For you have told me, '*...do not fear, for I am with you; do not be dismayed for I am your God. I will strengthen you and help you; I will uphold you with my right hand*'" (Isaiah 41:10).

Because He is with us we have no reason to feel hopeless. He is our God who at this time is saying, "*Here's hope. Just receive it. Receive Me for I want to be your very present help in times of trouble.*" After all, "*I am the Lord your God who takes hold of your right hand and says to you, 'Do not fear, I will help you'"* (Isaiah 41:13).

Now as the storms of life threaten you and you have troubles of many kinds, let Jesus take you in His arms. Lay your head on His chest listening to His heart beat, knowing that every beat is a communication of how much He loves you.

Remember *"God is not a man, so He does not lie. He is not human, so He does not change His mind. Has He ever spoken and failed to act? Has He ever promised and not carried it through?"* (Numbers 23:19).

God has a plan and purpose for your life. He has revealed it in many ways. The plans God has for your future are good plans. He says in Jeremiah 29:11, *"I know the plans I have for you. Plans to prosper you and not to harm you, plans to give you hope and a future."*

Even if you are in the midst of circumstances that seem to derail those plans continue to trust the Word of God.

Don't let discouragement swallow you up. God has good plans for you. They may be different than the plans you have but His are far better. They are plans that will give you a future filled with hope. Now receive the hope that Christ has for you at this time. He wants to perform the impossible through you. What God has in store for you is way outside your wildest dreams. The only thing that will restrain you from receiving God's miracles for your life is your hopelessness, fears and unbelief.

Listen to what He is telling you right now in Isaiah 40:30-31. *"Even youths will become weak and tired, and young men will fall in exhaustion. But those who trust in the Lord will find new strength. They will soar high on wings like eagles. They will run and not grow weary. They will walk and not faint."*

Aren't you tired of flapping your wings? The harder you flap, the more tired you become. It seems like you are getting nowhere. When will you start receiving the help Jesus has for you? Position yourself with Him. When you do that you will glide above the troubles that are wearing you down. You will soar to new heights. **As you trust in God you will find new strength and not grow weary and exhausted.**

Listen and obey as Jesus says, "*Come to me, all of you that are weary and are carrying heavy burdens and I will give you rest*" (Matthew 11:28).

Don't you love the sound of Jesus' invitation as he says, "Here's hope, here's rest for your body, mind and spirit. Just come to me let me help you."

To refuse His invitation is to go on struggling alone in a world filled with bad news, heartache, pain, sorrow, trouble and despair. As you live that way with each passing day you will get sucked further and further into feelings of hopelessness and depression.

When you start trusting in Jesus and receiving His help you will be filled with supernatural **joy**, **peace** and **hope**. It will begin to spill out of you until other people notice. Then you can tell them that this hope isn't anything about what you have done. It's about what **Jesus has done for you.** It is the power of His presence at work in your life.

Now is the time to turn on the spigot of hope that never runs dry. *"May the God of hope fill you with all joy and peace as you trust in Him, so that you may overflow with hope by the power of the Holy Spirit"* (Romans 15:13).

As you surrender your life, hopelessness, and worries to Jesus you will begin to discover that life can be awfully simple rather than simply awful. Then your heart will begin to leap for joy because the Lord will be your **strength** and **hope**. You will have peace of mind knowing He is your helper. As Psalm 28:7 says, *"The Lord is my strength and my shield; my heart trusts in Him, and He helps me. My heart leaps for joy, and with my song I praise Him."*

Praise the Lord. Every day with Him is a new day filled with hope. What an adventure life can become, as you trust in

Jesus and receive His help. When you do this you will see the miraculous unfold.

In the midst of hopelessness instead of panicking you will pray and obey when God says, *"Call upon Me and I will answer you and show you great and mighty things, fenced in and hidden, which you do not know (do not distinguish and recognize, have knowledge of and understand)"* (Jeremiah 33:3).

Although He will show me many things there still will be those times I do not understand. That is why I must accept the wisdom shared in verses like Proverbs 3:5-6. There it says, *"Trust in the Lord with all your heart, do not depend on your own understanding. Seek His will in all you do, and He will show you which path to take."*

As we seek the Lord God Almighty in all we do, trusting Him with all our heart, we will see that Christianity is not just a feel good religion. God never intended for His people to just be a bunch of happy-go-lucky people marching to heaven. He has called us forth to be a part of His revolution of love in this culture of hate.

As revolutionaries who open shelters for the homeless, seeing that everyone has a place to sleep and food to eat, we will make enemies. Jesus said if we were going to truly be His uncompromising followers in this bigoted culture of death we will have enemies.

When I see the enemies of the homeless and hurting ranting and raving that the homeless won't be sheltered in their neighborhood, I have hope. I know that ultimately God's powerful right hand will smash and overthrow those who come up against Christ's work as mandated in Matthew 25:31-46 and other places in scripture.

After the oppressive Egyptians were completely defeated Moses made this universal declaration. *"Your right hand O Lord, is glorious in power. Your right hand, O Lord smashes the enemy. In the greatness of your majesty you overthrow those who rise against you. You unleash your blazing fury, it consumes them like straw"* (Exodus 15:6-7).

God has not called us to hover in fear but to arise and move forth in faith, hope and love.

Our Lord is standing by to help as He declares, *"Who will rise up for me against the wicked? Who will take a stand for me against evil doers?"* (Psalm 94:16).

We always want God's help, now why won't we help those He has called every believer to help? This includes the poor, fatherless, widowed, sick, incarcerated and homeless. What excuses will we make on the last day concerning the locked doors of our hearts which should be filled with hope and compassion?

"Because of His great love for us, God, who is rich in mercy made us alive with Christ even when we were dead in trespasses. It is by grace you have been saved… for it is by grace you have been saved, through faith, and this is not from yourselves, it is a gift of God, not by works,

so that no one can boast. For we are God's handiwork, created in Christ Jesus to do good works, which God prepared in advance for us to do" (Ephesians 2:4-5,8-10).

There is hope. Christ is Risen. Now He is calling us as a redeemed people to help others who are in need. Let us move forth at this time as a people who have hope knowing that "...*we are more than conquerors through Christ who strengthens us*" (Romans 8:37).

Here's hope, now let it change your life by answering the following.

1. In light of Psalm 121:1-2 and Deuteronomy 31:8 where does hope for help in time of need come from?

2. What did Christ do to give us hope when we were utterly helpless according to Romans 5:6-8?

3. Why is prayer so important for maintaining hope as it is explained in Matthew 7:7-8?

4. What has God promised us in Isaiah 40:29 and why should this give you hope?

5. Jeremiah 29:11 tells you the plans God has for you. What are they?

6. What happens to those who trust in the Lord according to Isaiah 40:30-31?

7. Who is the spigot of hope who never runs dry and what will He fill you with according to Romans 15:13?

8. What is the promise given to you in Jeremiah 33:3?

9. Exodus 15:6-7 tells us what God will do in the majesty of His power. What is it?

10. According to Ephesians 2:4-5,8-10 what has God done for us and what does He prepare for us to do?

Living in Hope, Faith and Love

Chapter 15

If we do not live a life of *hope, faith* and *love* we will discover there are so many things we can be afraid of. We will fear crime, sickness, failure and the future. The list goes on and on. Fear will paralyze and destroy. Just look at the churches and communities that say they are afraid to help the homeless in their neighborhoods, because they fear the neighbors will object.

Daily we are presented with the choice of whether we are going to let fear or faith, hope or hopelessness or love and lovelessness rule our lives. If we are going to make an entry into a life of hope rather than fear, then we need to know how **hope, faith** and **love grows**. Romans 10:17 tells us, *"Faith comes from hearing the message, and the message is heard through the Word of Christ."*

Hope, faith and love can be ours even in the midst of battles for righteousness and justice as we keep our hearts and minds fixed on the love and hope that Jesus the author and finisher of our faith gives. For that reason, knowing Christ is there enables us to rejoice as Philippians 4:4-5 declares, *"Rejoice in the Lord always. I will say it again: Rejoice! Let your gentleness be evident to all. The Lord is near."*

The fact the Lord is near changes everything. It means I am not alone when it comes to confronting injustice. God is in control as 1 Kings 21 points out. There I see that at first it may appear that Ahab and Jezebel are the big winners when they take by eminent domain Naboth's property and then have him killed. But as I read the rest of 1 Kings 21 I see that Ahab and Jezebel end up being the big losers.

Even knowing this I find myself asking why are developers awarded tax abatements and the right to eminent domain resulting in the poor and elderly being put on the street without assistance? I have to ask what is wrong with a free market that doesn't create adequate affordable housing but yet promotes the conversion of apartments into condominiums and gentrifies neighborhoods by displacing low-income people? How can I as a believer not take a stand for justice, as neighborhoods are redlined by financial institutions so poor people and landlords providing low income housing can't get loans to fix their buildings? How can local governments say they want to eliminate chronic homelessness as they allow poor neighborhoods to deteriorate, in order that these communities can become candidates for urban renewal resulting in rents being raised above the ability of the poor and elderly to pay?

We are told in Amos 5:24, "*Let justice roll on like a river, righteousness like a never-failing stream.*" When you study Amos 5:21-24 you will see that the prophet Amos cries out that if our hope, faith and love does not bring justice flowing like a river, then we should stop the noise we are making at our religious gatherings. The reason for this is because God gets tired of hearing it, unless what we call praise is followed by acts of justice and compassion.

Homelessness is the end result of the Social Darwinism of the twenty-first century. There is no book, which more precisely addresses both the cause and solutions for homelessness than the Bible. In the Bible we find over 2,000 verses which relate to the poor. Although it points out how people can end up homeless as a result of wrong choices (see the story of the prodigal son) it also challenges those who claim to be the people of God to reach out to those in need.

Individuals that say they are followers of Jesus Christ need to reexamine His mission statement. Jesus said, *"The Spirit of the Lord is upon me because He has anointed me to preach good news to the poor. He has sent me to proclaim freedom for the prisoners and recovery of sight for the blind, to release the oppressed, to proclaim the year of the Lord's favor"* (Luke 4:18-19).

In order to preach the good news to the poor, proclaim freedom to prisoners, recovery of sight to the blind, and freedom to the oppressed, we must confront the greed, self-centeredness, and fear in our own lives. This is possible as we accept the Lord's favor and strive by His grace to live a life of **hope, faith** and **love**. As a result of the forgiveness of sins that Jesus Christ provided through His death and resurrection we can be liberated from this tyranny of sin. When this happens we are set free to ask the Holy Spirit to give us viable solutions to pursue Jesus' mission of proclaiming in word and deed good news to the poor and oppressed.

As we share **hope, faith** and **love** with others we are told in Philippians 4:6, "*Do not be anxious about anything, but in everything, by prayer and petition, with thanksgiving, present your requests to God.*"

I have learned that I will never be able to grasp the plain truth of this verse as I try to figure the how, when and where of the needed miracle. At some point I must turn loose of all the hopelessness related to the need I am facing. Instead of worrying I am required by this mandate of Scripture to **take the need to God in prayer.**

Accepting the reality that the love of God, demonstrated through the resurrected Christ, extends to the issues of homelessness and social injustice, releases hope, faith and love within me. **This frees me from my anxiety and allows me to pray.** This is not a form of escapism but a new understanding that through prayer I am able to cast all my anxiety and hopelessness on the Lord.

Matthew 6:31-34 promises us *"Therefore do not worry, saying, 'What shall we eat?' or 'What shall we drink?' or 'What shall we wear?' For after all these things the Gentiles seek. For your heavenly Father knows that you need all these things. But seek first the kingdom of God and His righteousness, and all these things shall be added to you. Therefore do not worry about tomorrow, for tomorrow will worry about its own things. Sufficient for the day is its own trouble."*

As I strive to live a life of **hope**, **faith** and **love** I am constantly reminded in scriptures like Psalm 82:3 to, *"Defend the* *poor and fatherless: do justice to the afflicted and needy."* As I read Scriptures like that, I must seek God through prayer as to what decisive action I am to take to help those in need. This includes feeding the hungry, sheltering the homeless and letting the love of God flow through me. Knowledge of the need is not enough. As 1 Corinthians 8:1 says, *"...knowledge puffs up, but love builds up."*

Some religious people will say it's not the job of the government to take care of the homeless and see they get justice. These individuals argue it is the job of the church. If that is the case, then show me the love in the churches that will let the homeless use their bathrooms and provide other direct help. After all didn't Jesus say, *"...as often as you have done it to the least of these even so you have done it unto me"* (Matthew 25:40).

When are we going to let Jesus come back into our churches? This will happen as we hear Him tell us to rise up and walk and be healed of the paralysis of fear. Then not only will we start asking the hard questions about justice for the homeless but we will begin demonstrating the **hope, faith** and **love** necessary to let the **love of Christ flow through us into the lives of those in need.**

Demonstrating such courage is not easy. As I stand steadfast and absorb the reality of God's presence manifested through the wonders of His works of creation, the inspired words of Scripture, and the anointing of the Holy Spirit, God's hope, faith and love begin to flood my troubled mind. This gives me firm assurance that Christ is present and God's love will prevail. Romans 8:28 reminds us, *"And we know that all things work together for good to those who love God, to those who are called according to His purpose."*

The reason we share **hope, faith** and **love** with the hurting and homeless is because God is a **God of compassion**. *"For the needy shall not always be forgotten, and the expectation and <u>hope</u> of the meek and the poor shall not perish forever"* (Psalm 9:18).

The Word of God, commonly referred to as the Bible, could also be called the book of **hope**, **faith** and **love**. In it we find the promises, power and presence of God affirmed over and over. We are told to, *"Trust in the Lord forever; for in the Lord God is an everlasting strength"* (Isaiah 26:4).

To trust in the Lord means to have faith in God. Hebrews 11:1 says, *"Faith is the substance of things <u>hoped</u> for."* Also Hebrews 11:6 says, *"Without faith it is impossible to please God."*

It is easy to lose **hope**, **faith** and **love**, when day after day all we see are people who feel they are in hopeless situations. We try to help them, but it never seems to be enough. How easy it is to let depression creep into our lives until even our future seems to be one of hopelessness. That is why it is so critical that we immerse ourselves in scriptures like Jeremiah 29:11, *"For I know the thoughts and plans that I have for you, says the Lord, thoughts and plans for welfare and peace and not for evil, to give you hope and a future."*

May God indeed awaken us in order that we can know and understand this hope that Ephesians 1:18 speaks of: *"The eyes of your understanding being enlightened; that you may know what is the hope of His calling, what are the riches of the glory of His inheritance to the saints."* When we do this *"We have this hope as an anchor for the soul"* (Hebrews 6:19).

This anchor of *"…hope does not disappoint us, because God has poured out His love into our hearts by the Holy Spirit, whom He has given us"* (Romans 5:5). It's a fact, hope centered in God and His promises is what will anchor us in the middle of the storms of life.

Even the trials, tribulations and afflictions we suffer on a day by day basis can serve to build **hope**, **faith** and **love** within us as we look to our Risen Savior. 2 Corinthians 4:17-18 says, *"For our light affliction, which is but for a moment, is working for us a far more exceeding and eternal weight of glory, while we do not look at the things which are seen, but at the things which are not seen. For the things* *which are seen are temporary, but the things which are not seen are eternal."*

Glory be to God! Because of **His infinite love**, **mercy** and **grace** we are people who can live in **hope**, **faith** and **love** both **now** and for all **eternity**. Yes, there may be hopeless circumstances but we are reminded that we are to *"Wait and hope for and expect the Lord; be brave and of good courage and let your heart be stout and enduring. Yes, wait for and hope for and expect the Lord"* (Psalm 27:14).

As you wait, *"May the God of hope fill you with all joy and peace as you trust in Him so that you may overflow with hope by the power of the Holy Spirit"* (Romans 15:13). The key to experiencing this joy and peace is to have **faith in the God of hope.** As you trust in Him you will overflow with hope and love by the power of the Holy Spirit.

Hope, faith and **love** is the **oxygen for our souls.** Now, may we continue to have faith in the God of hope and let His love flow through us until we become His light in what seems like a hopeless dark world. As this happens we will see our Lord and Savior Jesus Christ do exceedingly far beyond what we can ask or think.

Complete the following and then let the hope, faith and love work in your life.

1. How does faith come alive in us according to Romans 10:17?

2. Why is living in hope, faith and love so critical when it comes to being God's instrument of justice and compassion among the poor and homeless?

3. What was Jesus' mission statement according to Luke 4:18-19?

4. How can we have hope our needs will be met in light of Matthew 6:31-34?

5. What command does Psalm 82:3 give us?
6. Psalm 9:18 makes a promise. What is it?

7. What does Hebrews 11:1 and Hebrews 11:6 have to say about faith?

8. Hope is more than wishful thinking. It is knowing the plans God has for us. What are they according to Jeremiah 29:11?

9. What is the benefit of affliction as explained in 2 Corinthians 4:17-18?

10. Seven directives are given in Psalm 27:14 for us to allow hope, faith and love in our life. What are they?

Finding Hope in Hopeless Dark Places
Chapter 16

What we see in the natural realm is what is also seen in the spiritual world. This is because both are woven together. In John 12:24 Jesus says, *"Most assuredly, I say to you, unless a grain of wheat falls into the ground and dies, it remains alone; but if it dies, it produces much grain."*

The fact is, it is hard being a seed in the ground. It is dark and seems hopeless there. Yet Jesus said unless we like seeds are buried in what seems like hopeless places, we can't produce much fruit or grain.

When a loved one dies, or a person gets a divorce, or ends up homeless, they naturally find themselves alone, and buried in hopeless lonely places.

The challenge is how we, like seeds, germinate in those lonely dark hopeless places. When we find ourselves like seeds buried in dark places we tend to rush for something, anything to fill the brokenness and hopelessness. When we do this, we miss what God desires to do in our lives.

We may at times feel lost in the loneliness of the dirty places. When that happens, we must remember we are not alone and hopeless. Christ is with us and He has also sent the Comforter, the Holy Spirit, and the angels, to directly assist us as they convert those hopeless places into good nourishing soil with hope.

In the midst of the dirty places, we must take seriously our angelic inheritance described in verses like Psalm 91:9-12 where it says, *"If you make the Most High your dwelling – even the Lord, who is my refuge – then no harm will befall you, no disaster will come near your tent. For He will command His angels concerning you to guard you in all your ways; they will lift you up in their hands, so that you will not strike your foot against a stone."*

It is hope in the fact God will protect us which turns the lonely hopeless places into nurturing soil filled with the hope of the certainty of divine help. This hope is broadcast to us daily through the wonders of creation.

<u>There are five sources of the hope we learn from creation.</u>

1. **God's Faithfulness.**

    As we observe creation we experience God's eternal presence, and are awakened to God's Faithfulness and the hope He gives. He is the God of hope as Romans 15:13 declares: *"May the God of hope fill you with all joy and peace as you trust in Him, so that you may overflow with hope by the power of the Holy Spirit."*

    This hope is demonstrated not only through the wonders of creation but also through the Scriptures, which tells us that God has sent His Son Jesus. It is Jesus, the resurrected Christ, who sends the Holy Spirit. The Holy Spirit helps us plow daily through our hopeless circumstances, planting seeds of life and hope.

2. **Hope comes through trusting Christ.**

    Because Christ is risen, we have hope as we trust in Him. The reality of Christ's resurrection is demonstrated through every seed that is planted and then resurrected into a wonderful plant with the purpose planned at the time of its creation.

As I strive to live as a new creation in Christ, I find myself awakened to the wonders of God's creation that "...*the world's a huge stockpile of God-wonders and God-thoughts*" (Psalm 40:5). As I walk through the wonders of God's creation I will not hear the birds sing, feel the refreshing breezes, see the wonderful sunsets, touch or smell all that He has created for me today unless I stop worrying and live in the present. The hurts of the past and the fears of the future will block out God's blessings of the present unless I live now with hope.

3. Hope helps us remember all that God has done for us.

When I go on my prayer walks I remember what God has done in the past and what He promises for the future. I then begin to pray using my senses of seeing, hearing, touching, smelling and tasting. Using my senses adds so much more to praying than just speaking words. Such praying challenges me to further focus on God and the wonders of His creation. As I pray I want my ears to hear the birds and other sounds of creation. I will frequently smell the flowers and even taste a leaf or even a flower. Then as I pray, I touch a tree and let the touch of the wind embrace me. Then my eyes are used to observe that squirrel, deer and other forms of wildlife as well as the beauty of the flowers, tree leaves, sunsets and much more.

Praying with the senses causes me to praise God and literally rise above my troubling thoughts and see that **God is bigger** than any problem. Bonaventure wrote, "*Concerning the mirror of things* *perceived through sensation, we can see God not only through them as through vestiges, but also in them, as He is in them by His essence, power, and presence…We are led to contemplate God in all creation which enter our mind through our bodily senses."*

When I think about God, as my bodily senses awaken to His presence, I begin to experience the fourth source for hope.

4. Hope grows as we depend on God in difficult times.

Our Creator gives us hope through His creation and the power of His word, *"Do not fear; for I am with you; do not be dismayed, for I am your God. I will strengthen you and help you; I will uphold you with my righteous right hand"* (Isaiah 41:10).

The fact that God upholds us with His righteous right hand tells us we **do not need to be afraid.**

The present circumstances cannot suffocate our hope for a future, for the resurrected Christ has provided hope both now and for all eternity.

Anyone who was previously dead in their hopelessness, fear, and sins, can now start all over because of the gift of hope that Christ provides. Believers today, who have received the hope Christ gives, have died to themselves and are now resurrected with Christ Jesus. That's why 2 Corinthians 5:17 says, *"If anyone be in Christ they are a new creation. The old has passed away and the new has come."*

5. **Hope grows as we remember the Resurrection and as a result we are a new creation.**

As a new creation in Christ I have the power to be set free from the memories and the worries that will enslave me. When I get all wrapped up in the memories of the past or the worries of the future I am not able to experience God's hope in the present.

Worry keeps me from experiencing the hope that God's creation provides daily. **Worry fills me so full of self that there is no room for God.** When there is no room for God there is no room for other people. As a result, worry and fear can drive me to hopelessness, or a self-centered spirituality, that does not include the needs of others. That is why I must spend time daily with the Lord in prayer, Bible reading, and the study of creation.

As I do this God's gift of hope will begin to take root in my life. I will begin to understand what it is to be a new creature in Christ, and live in the newness and power He provides.

There is so much we can learn from creation. All of creation, including the mountains, the trees, and the waters, are God's temple. We need them for our own spiritual health. By reflecting on the redemptive work of Christ, and how all things were created by Him, and how He holds all things together, we cannot help but see the sacredness of creation. *"He is the image of the invisible God, the firstborn over all creation. For by Him all things were created; things in heaven and on earth, visible and invisible, whether thrones or powers or rulers or authorities; all things were created by Him and for Him. He is before all things and in Him all things hold together"* (Colossians 1:15-17).

As we look to Christ, the first born of all creation, hope will come alive within us, even in the dark lonely places. Then our heart and mind will open up to the needs of others as we let the love of God flow through us. It is then that the hopelessness can be transformed into nourishing soil of hope. As this happens the seed of God's love will germinate in the nourishing soil in us and forgiveness and love will sprout in our lives. In this nourishing soil of hope we will relax and trust Jesus when He says,

"Lo, I am with you always even to the end of the world" (Matthew 28:20).

Breaking through the hopelessness where we are planted enables us to arise and see the great opportunities God has placed before us. As this happens we will see the hopelessness changed into hope where we can grow and be used for the Glory of God.

Jesus promised we would not be alone in our hopeless circumstances. He would be with us always even to the end of the world. In addition, Jesus has promised to send his comforter, the Holy Spirit. There are also the angels, those wonderful ministering spirits who are available to those who will inherit salvation.

In Luke 18:7-8 Jesus tells us, *"And will not God bring about justice for His chosen ones, who cry out to Him day and night? Will He keep putting them off? I tell you, He will see that they get justice and quickly. However, when the Son of Man comes, will He find faith on the earth?"*

It is our loving heavenly father who transforms hopelessness into

hope. It is there we experience Romans 8:28 which says, "*We know that in all things God works for the good of those who love him, who have been called according to His purpose.*" Let us rejoice in the reality of this promise of hope, knowing that wherever we are planted, Jesus will never leave us nor forsake us.

Dig in and answer the questions below to find hope in hopeless places.

1. What hope is given while being in a dark hopeless place in John 12:24?

2. A promise is given to produce hope in Psalm 91:9-12. What is it?

3. What are the 5 sources of hope we learn from creation?

4. According to Bonaventure how do we contemplate God in all of creation?

5. What reasons do we have not to fear according to Isaiah 41:10?

6. 2 Corinthians 5:17 tells us something happens to a person who is in Christ. What is it?

7. How does worry keep us from experiencing the hope that God's creation provides daily?

8. Who is Christ according to Colossians 1:15-17?

9. How does breaking through the hopelessness where we are planted allow us to see the opportunities God has placed before us?

10. What promise and what question is given in Luke 18:7-8?

Jesus the Hope of Heaven
Chapter 17

The hope we have available through Jesus is not only for this life but for all eternity. That is why we can say that Jesus is the Hope of Heaven.

1 Peter 1:13 tells us, "*...therefore preparing your minds for action, and being sober minded set your hope fully on the grace that will be brought to you at the revelation of Jesus Christ.*"

Jesus tells us the basis for this hope in John 14:1-3. There He declares, "*Do not let your hearts be trouble. You believe in God; believe also in me. My Father's house has many rooms; if that were not so, would I have told you that I am going there to prepare a place for you? And if I go and prepare a place for you, I will come back and take you to be with me that you also may be where I am.*"

Jesus became the Homeless One, leaving His home in heaven in order that He might come to earth to gather you and I, as

His homeless children, and take us to be with Him forever in heaven.

What a glorious day that will be when we get to our home in heaven. But for now we must get ready for the trip there. With each passing day, we get closer and closer to our home in heaven. The promise of heaven, because of the death and resurrection of Christ, provides us with hope no matter what difficulties this life presents.

Peter J. Kreeft in his book called "Heaven" writes, "It is unreasonable (and in fact escapist) not to plan for a trip to Australia before you go, especially if it is a one-way trip. But the trip to heaven or hell is surer, longer, and more certainly one-way than a trip to Australia. For every earthly trip, you at least make some inquiries at the travel bureau. The church claims to be the heavenly travel bureau as well as the ship, the Noah's ark, in which we go. Simply to ignore this claim as escapism is the sheerest escapism. The escapism of worldliness is compounded by the fact that we are already embarked on our journey to the other world. As soon as we are born, we begin to die. This world is like a rocket ship; we are already launched into the beyond. Life is an escalator, and there is no way off except at the end. The only choice is between directions: up or down."

"Those of us who hope to go up to our home in heaven are told, '*Let us throw off everything that hinders and the sin that so easily entangles, and let us run with perseverance the race marked out for us*' (Hebrews 12:1). Running this race is only possible through the grace that the death and resurrection of Jesus Christ gives us."

"2 Corinthians 5:1 says, '*If your earthly house, this tent, is destroyed, we have a building from God, a house not made with hands, eternal in the heavens.*' Isaiah 26:19 also says, '*But your dead will live, Lord; their bodies will rise—let those who dwell in the dust wake up and shout for joy—your dew is like the dew of the morning; the earth will give birth to her dead.*'"

"Life is very fragile. We never know when we will die. Facing this reality, our prayers should be, '*Teach us to number our days aright, that we may gain a heart of wisdom*" (Psalm 90:12). This heart of wisdom involves receiving the free life insurance policy Jesus gives and learning how to let go of this world. This letting go, or disengaging can seem painful, but in reality it provides the freedom necessary to really live. It involves seeing death, not as the end, but as the doorway to a new life; which is now possible because of the death and resurrection of Jesus Christ. In Hebrews 2:14-15, we read, "*So that by His death He (Jesus) might destroy him who holds the power of death—that is the devil—and free those who all their lives were held in slavery by their fear of death.*"

Peter J. Kreeft goes on to say that as we travel through life, we need a purpose for living. "Living for no reason is more tragic than dying for a reason, for living for no reason is not living, but mere existing, mere surviving. As Viktor Frank found in a Nazi concentration camp, our deepest rock-bottom need is not pleasure, as Freud thought, or power, as Adler thought, but meaning and purpose, 'a reason to live and a reason to die.' We need a meaning to life more than we need life itself."

It is the fear of death which prevents us from really living. When we realize that death is not the end, but only the beginning, then we are free to take the necessary risks that come from living courageous lives. We will discover as we live such lives freed from the slavery of the fear of death that God meant what He said in Jeremiah 29:11, *"For I know the plans I have for you,"* declares the Lord, *"plans to prosper you and not harm you, plans to give you hope and a future."* Paul, who was looking forward to going home to heaven declared, *"For to me, to live is Christ and to die is gain"* (Philippians 1:21).

Those who refuse to accept Jesus' invitation to go home to the heaven that He provided through His death and resurrection, have every reason to fear death. Instead of an eternity in the presence of the Living God, who is love, what awaits the unbeliever is condemnation and an eternal separation from God. "*Whoever believes in Him is not condemned, but whoever does not believe stands condemned already because he has not believed in the name of God's one and only Son*" (John 3:18).

Billy Graham in his book, "Nearing Home," shares the following: "We sometimes speak of a beautiful sunset or a warm spring day as 'glorious,' but even earth's most awe-inspiring nature is but a shadow of the glory of heaven. When the apostle John was given a glimpse of heaven's grandeur, he barely could find words to describe it, comparing it to the most wondrous objects on earth—only far greater: '*It shone with the glory of God, and its brilliance was like that of a very precious jewel, like a jasper, clear as crystal…The great street of the city was of pure gold, like transparent glass…This city does not need the sun or the moon to shine on it, for the glory of God gives it light, and the Lamb [Christ] is its lamp*' (Revelation 21:11,21,23)."

He goes on to say, "Why is heaven glorious? It isn't simply because of its incredible beauty, overwhelming as that will be. Heaven is glorious for one supreme reason: Heaven is the dwelling place of God. *'And I heard a loud voice from the throne saying, "Now the dwelling of God is with men, and He will live with them. They will he His people, and God himself will be with them and be their God...They will see His face, and His name will be on their foreheads"* (Revelation 21:3; 22:4). Think of it: if you know Jesus Christ, someday you will be safely in God's presence forever! I can barely imagine what that will be like—but it will be glorious beyond description."

What a wonderful place heaven will be! *"For the trumpet will sound, the dead will be raised imperishable, and we will be changed. For the perishable must clothe itself with the imperishable and the mortal with immortality. When the perishable has been clothed with the imperishable, and the mortal with immortality, then the saying that is written will come true: 'Death has been swallowed up in victory, where, O death, is your sting?' The sting of death is sin, and the power of sin is the law. But thanks be to God! He gives us the victory through our Lord Jesus Christ"* (1 Corinthians 15:52-57).

1 Corinthians 2:9 says, *"No eye has seen, nor ear has heard, no mind has conceived what God has prepared for those who love Him."* Jonathon Edwards, trying to explain the awesomeness of our home in heaven declared, "To pretend to describe the excellence, the greatness or duration of the happiness of heaven by the artful composition of words would be but to darken and cloud it; to talk of raptures and ecstasies, joy and singing, is but to set forth very low shadows of reality."

Jesus, desiring that everyone would come to heaven, died on the cross to provide the forgiveness of sins necessary to go there. He rose from the dead and now declares we too shall live for all eternity with Him in heaven, if we but believe and receive the eternal life He provides. *"For our citizenship is in heaven, from which we also eagerly wait for the Savior, the Lord Jesus Christ, who will transform our lowly body that it may be conformed to His glorious body, according the working by which He is able even to subdue all things to Himself"* (Philippians 3:20 & 21).

Knowing that I am going home to heaven changes everything. I know my stay on this earth is temporary, and because of what Christ has done for me, I want to serve Him with my total being. As a believer who is going home to heaven, I receive a taste of heaven now as the Holy Spirit works within me and awakens me daily to the wonders of God's creation. With this taste of heaven, my hope keeps growing as I look forward to go there with each passing day.

C.S. Lewis wrote, "There have been times when I think we do not desire heaven, but more often, I find myself wondering whether, in our heart of hearts, we have ever desired anything else…Your place in heaven will seem to be made for you and you alone, because you were made for it stitch by stitch, as a glove made for a hand."

Living in the light of eternity and knowing you are going home to heaven means being filled with hope and love for others. "*We know that we have passed from death to life, because we love the brethren. He who does not love his brothers (or sisters) abides in death. Whoever hates his brother (or sister) is a murderer, and you know that no murderer has eternal life abiding in him. By this we know love, because He laid down His life for us. And we also ought to lay down our lives for the brethren. But whoever has this world's goods, and sees his brother (or sister) in need, and shuts up his heart from him (or her), how does the love of God abide in him? Let us not love in word or tongue, but in deed and in truth*" (1 John 3:14-18).

As we let the love of God flow through us in deed and truth, with the hope of heaven at work in us, we will want to tell everyone about Jesus. God wanted humanity in heaven so badly that "*He sent His only begotten Son that whosoever believeth in Him shall not perish but have everlasting life*" (John 3:16).

In Revelation 22:3-5 we read about this heavenly city that God has prepared for those who believe in Jesus and have accepted the forgiveness of sins He provides. *"No longer will there be any curse. The throne of God and the Lamb will be in the city, and His servants will serve Him. They will see His face and His name will be on their foreheads. There will be no more light. They will not need the light of a lamp or the light of the sun, for the Lord God will give them light. And they will reign forever and ever."*

Randy Alcorn reflecting on this ultimate reward made the following observation about Heaven. "Christ centered righteous living today is directly affected by knowing where we're going and what rewards we'll receive there for serving Christ… Following Christ is not a call to abstain from gratification but to delay gratification. It is finding our joy in Christ rather than seeking joy in the things of this world. Heaven – our assurance of external gratification and fulfillment should be our North Star, reminding us where we are and which direction to go. When we realize the pleasures that await us in God's presence, we can forego lesser pleasures now. When we realize the possessions that await us in Heaven, we will gladly give away possessions on Earth to store up treasures in Heaven."

If we are going to talk about heaven then let's discuss why so many people who say they are going there are intent on gathering as much stuff as they can on the journey. It makes as much sense as a homeless person pushing three or four carts of stuff up and down the streets knowing that when they get to the shelter at night they can't take those things in with them. Now let's remember the place or the shelter Jesus said in John 14:2 He was going to prepare for us. The fact is when the time comes for us to go to that shelter we have to go through the door of death. Since no one ever takes their stuff through that door why is it that so many who claim they are going to leave spend so much time and money on gathering stuff that they could spend helping others?

Jesus lays it out straight in Matthew 6:19-21 when he says, "***Do not store up for yourselves treasures on earth***, *where moths and rust destroy, and where thieves break in and steal. But store up for yourselves treasures in heaven, where moths and rust do not destroy, and where thieves do not break in and steal. For where your treasure is, there your heart will be also."*

While we are here on earth let us use every opportunity God has given us to directly help those in need for our labor in the Lord is not in vain. Revelation 14:13 says, "*…I heard a voice from heaven saying, 'Write this down: Blessed are those who die in the Lord from now on. Yes, says the Spirit, they are blessed indeed, for they will rest from their hard work; for their good deeds follow them.'"*

As Ephesians 2:8-10 says, "***For it is by grace you have been saved, through faith****—and this is not from yourselves, it is the gift of God—not by works, so that no one can boast. For we are God's handiwork, created in Christ Jesus to do* *good works, which God prepared in advance for us to do."*

I stood on the promise of this scripture as I stood at the foot of my sister's grave and then again when my father died as when my first wife Penny did, and later my mother. Each time I found hope in the fact that my loved ones had experienced the victory given through Jesus Christ and that someday I would be in heaven with them.

The hope of this victory after death affects the way we live and work in the here and now. Before such certainty existed, we were unstable, purposeless and hopeless. But now because of Christ's work on the cross and His resurrection which followed we have hope. As a result, Paul's directive for our daily lives makes sense when he says, *"Stand firm. Let nothing move you. Always give yourselves fully to the work of the Lord because you know that your labor in the Lord is not in vain"* (1 Corinthians 15:58).

See for yourself the hope waiting for you in heaven as you answer the following.

1. What are we supposed to set our hope on according to 1 Peter 1:13?

2. Jesus tells us the basis for this hope in John 14:1-3. What is it?

3. How does Peter J. Kreeft explain that we are to sift our hope from this life to heaven by "learning how to let go of this world"?

4. Jeremiah 29:11 tells us that God has "plans to give you hope and a future." How does this relate to the hope and future of heaven?

5. What promise and warning is given in John 3:18?

6. According to Billy Graham why is heaven glorious?

7. In light of Philippians 3:20-21 what will Jesus do with our present bodies?

8. Describe heaven according to Revelation 22:3-5.

9. How does 1 Corinthians 15:52-57 describe what a wonderful place heaven will be?

10. Because of the hope we have for heaven what directives does Paul give us in 1 Corinthians 15:58 for how we are to live now?

A Haven of Hope

New Life Evangelistic Center is a haven of hope for the hopeless and homeless. Because of its thousands of faithful partners, new NCEC is able to share the hope provided through the Risen Christ around the clock. This is done through direct help centers, homeless outreach search and rescue teams, broadcast and social media sites.

This book you are holding in your hands is a result of just two of the multitude of lives you are offering hope to as you partner with NLEC. Julie who typed "Living In Hope" shares the following:

I have discovered a new hope within myself. When I first came to New Life Evangelistic Center, I was initially searching for a place to stay. I was homeless with nowhere to go and felt lost. After moving into a safe house and becoming part of this community I now have the opportunity to serve Jesus Christ on a daily basis. My new purpose is to share the Good News of God and His resurrected Son through Bible study, prayer, outreach and living in hope. This is so much more than just a place to stay, it is my oasis of hope! Julie

I found myself sleeping in the doorway of the church near my Grandmother's house because I had nowhere else to go to lay my head. I would sleep with one eye open because there was a huge raccoon that seemed to want to get close to me! I tried to get into shelters, but found I had a very difficult time because everyone was FULL! There were no beds at the Inn available to me. Finally, I was able to find the rest and freedom from homelessness that I needed through the New Life Evangelistic Center Residential Leadership Program. I have grown closer to my Savior, Jesus Christ, and found peace from my troubles here at New Life Evangelistic Center. Deborah

For more information on the work of New Life Evangelistic Center please go to www.newlifeevangelisticcenter.org. If you need help or desire to become a part of the worldwide world of NLEC please write New Life Evangelistic Center, P.O. Box 473, St. Louis, MO 63166, or call 314-421-3020.

Made in the USA
Monee, IL
11 June 2024